GROUP THERAPY

SELF-AWARENESS

Suzanne M. Howard
Board Certified Mental Health Coach,
AACC

Battle Press
SATELLITE BEACH, FLORIDA

Group Therapy
Self-Awareness

Copyright © 2022 by Suzanne M. Howard

Books may be ordered through booksellers or by contacting:

Suzanne M. Howard
suzhoward@yahoo.com
www.suzannemhoward.com

Or

Battle Press
steve@battlepress.media
battlepress.media
919-218-4039

Because of the dynamic nature of the internet, any web addresses or links contained in this book may have changed since publication and may no longer be valid.

ISBN: 979-8-9862-6328-1 (SC)
ISBN: 979-8-9862-6329-8 (eBook

LCCN: 2022919070

First Edition.

TABLE OF CONTENTS

DEDICATION

I dedicate this book to my son Larry and my granddaughter Payton; I love you both dearly!

I wish above all things that you prosper and be in good health even as your soul prospers!

Self-Awareness & Self-Love
are not given they are grown.

ABOUT THE AUTHOR

Suzanne M. Howard is a Certified Mental Health Coach, speaker, Pastor, founder of suzannemhoward.com Coaching, and author of Group Therapy, Self, a series of self-help and personal development books.

Suzanne has over a decade of writing curriculums and sermons and speaking throughout the New England region and beyond. She has turned a personal journey into a much broader influence of helping others through their journey. Being a teenage mother, Suzanne has fought, failed, and won many battles. She is devoted to her faith and her lifelong mission to help others overcome their soul issues. She resides in Connecticut with her husband, son, and granddaughter.

Suzanne is available for group workshops and one-on-one coaching or mentoring sessions. To learn more please check her out at

suzannemhoward.com

psychologytoday.com

INTRODUCTION

T o know thyself is the beginning of wisdom." -Socrates

Do you want to be happier, have more influence, be a better decision-maker, and be a more effective leader? Self-awareness, then, is the most important muscle you need to develop. It's what will keep you on target to be the best version of yourself and the best leader you can be.

On a scale of 1-10, how self-aware do you think you are?

If you don't know how to answer this question, you aren't alone. One study estimates that only 10-15% of people are truly self-aware.

If self-awareness is so important, why do so many people struggle with it, let alone understand what it means?

A big reason is that we live in a world where we are conditioned to operate on autopilot.

This busy mindset doesn't leave room for much self-reflection and introspection. By not taking the time to connect with ourselves, we stop paying attention to what is going on internally. As you can imagine, this can be a recipe for an emotional disaster.

Self-awareness is one of the pivotal life skills. Imagine being a lovely flower with a wonderful fragrance, but you're not able to realize your beauty! How different could your life be if you were aware of your beauty? This is the role of self-awareness in our lives: to teach us our hidden reality. Unfortunately, not everyone cares about this issue, because only a few realize its importance, and most of us focus on others rather than ourselves.

Self-awareness is the foundation for personal growth. It involves understanding your own needs, desires, failings, habits, and everything else that makes you tick.

If you want to strive to be a better person, you need to get intimate with yourself, meaning you've got to know who you are and who you are not. Moreover, you've got to be able to accurately monitor your inner world, as well as accept who you are with an open heart.

This is where a lot of people get stuck.

It takes courage to go deep with yourself and look at messy emotions that you don't necessarily want to acknowledge, let alone work on. Let's face it... growth isn't always pretty. It sometimes feels like an uphill climb. However, it is the one thing that is required if you want to level up your life and become more of who you want to be.

CHAPTER ONE
WHAT IS SELF-AWARENESS?

How well do you know yourself? If you're like most people, you're probably familiar with the basics: You like this, hate that, and have a knack for a certain skill. But what about your behaviors and thoughts—and how they affect your life? You know, the deep stuff.

That's where self-awareness comes in.

So, what is self-awareness?

Simply put, it is the act and process of observing yourself, and how you interact with your environment, including situations and other people. It involves noticing and acknowledging how things impact you and vice versa. In other words, it is an interactive, two-way process of noticing influence and impact.

Self-awareness is the ability to focus on yourself and how your actions, thoughts, or emotions do or don't align with your internal standards. If you're highly self-aware, you can objectively evaluate yourself, manage your emotions, align your behavior with your values, and understand correctly how others perceive you.

At its basic level, self-awareness is the ability to understand that the self is separate from others; however, to be self-aware, a person must be able to recognize and label their feelings, thoughts, and behaviors. If a person is self-aware, they can assess their physical, mental, and emotional states and understand there are various aspects of their internal personality that allow them to interact with the external world.

At its core, self-awareness showcases that a person is separate from others regarding thoughts, wants, and needs. On a broader scale, self-awareness allows a person to answer the following questions:

- Who am I?

- What do I want now or in the future?

- What should I do next?

- What do I think about a particular topic/situation?

- How do I feel (physically and emotionally) right now?

If a person can answer these questions, it shows they are self-aware because they understand their physical and emotional needs in connection to the world around them. Being able to answer these questions encompasses the self-awareness definition and the self-awareness meaning.

Self-awareness is one of the first components of the self-concept to emerge. While self-awareness is central to who you are, it is not something that you are acutely focused on at every moment of every day. Instead, self-awareness becomes woven into the fabric of who you are and emerges at different points depending on the situation and your personality.

Self-awareness is about looking at who you are in a way that acknowledges how you impact others [and] how they impact you. It also involves understanding your emotions and internal narrative, allowing you to lead a fulfilling life. "It's the first step to changing and growing,"

Put simply, those who are highly self-aware can interpret their actions, feelings, and thoughts objectively. It's a rare skill, as many of us spiral into emotion-driven interpretations of our circumstances. Developing self-awareness is important because it allows leaders to assess their growth and effectiveness and change course when necessary.

Self-awareness is being aware of oneself that includes ones traits, feelings, behavior. It is quite difficult in today's time to find time to think about who we are, what are our strengths and weaknesses, our personalities, our habits, and our values. Besides, many of us are not just inclined to spend much time on self-reflection. Consequently, many of us have a low level of self-awareness because self-awareness is an essential first step toward maximizing management skills. It can improve our judgment and help us identify opportunities for professional development and personal growth.

Key Areas for Self-Awareness include our personality traits, personal values, habits, emotions, psychological needs.

i. Personality

It has been said that personalities cant be changed. As a follower of Jesus The Christ, I believe we can become new and that personalities can be altered by awareness, desire to change and growth. Understanding our personality can help us find in what environment we can sustain. Awareness of our personality helps us analyze such a decision.

For instance, if you are a highly introverted person, you are likely to experience more stress in a sales position than a highly extroverted person would. So, if you are highly introverted, you should either learn skills to cope with the demands of a sales position that requires extravert-type behavior patterns, or you should find a position that is more compatible with your personality. Awareness of your personality helps you analyze such a decision.

ii. Values

It's important that we know and focus on our values. When we focus on our values, we are more likely to accomplish what we consider most important.

iii. Habits

Our habits are the behaviors that we repeat daily and often automatically. Although we would like to possess the habits that help us interact effectively with and manage others, we can probably all identify with at least one of our habits that decrease our effectiveness.

iv. Needs

Scholars have identified a variety of psychological needs that drive our behaviors such as needs for esteem, affection, belongingness, achievement, self-actualization, power, and control.

v. Emotions

It's one of the five facets of emotional intelligence. Understanding your feelings, what causes them, and how they impact our thoughts and actions is emotional self-awareness. A person with high emotional self-awareness understands the internal process associated with emotional experiences and, therefore, has greater control over them.

More specifically, self-awareness is about observing:

- **Patterns of thought.** How do you tend to think about and explain what happens to you? What's your self-talk like? What expectations do you hold in certain settings or with certain people? What are your core beliefs that influence your thinking?

- **Patterns of emotion.** How well do you understand your moods and emotions? Do you observe and try to understand your emotions or do you react to them impulsively? Do you view difficult emotions as enemies to be avoided or gotten rid of or messengers trying to tell you something?

- **Patterns of behavior.** Do you understand why you tend to act in the same way in certain situations? Do you have a sense of what types of events are triggering for you? Do you understand what motivates your behaviors or leads to self-sabotage?

TYPES OF SELF-AWARENESS

Being self-aware means being in tune with your emotions, feelings, state of mind, motives, and desires.

Dr. Tasha Eurich, self-awareness expert and best-selling author of "Insight: The Surprising Truth About How Others See Us, How We See Ourselves, and Why the Answers Matter More Than We Think", discovered that 95% of people think they are self-aware, but only about 15% of people really are.

There's a disconnect between how aware we think we are of our emotions and the truth.

Dr. Eurich says there are two types of self-awareness: internal and external.

Internal self-awareness is how we see our values, thoughts, and emotions. To practice this, move away from asking why. Instead of asking "Why did I say that to a team member?", ask yourself "What made me say that to my team member?" You can't always rationalize the why, but you can always explain the what.

Essentially, internal self-awareness is recognizing your current job doesn't match your true passion for marketing, or feeling dissatisfied with a heated conversation you had with your colleague, which conflicts with your belief that kindness is important.

External self-awareness is how we are seen by others. To practice this, create an open and safe environment where team members and peers can be honest with you. Encourage critical feedback that ultimately helps you improve.

Interestingly, Eulrich's research has found no link between these two types. Someone with high internal self-awareness and low external self-awareness might be particularly introspective and rarely seek outside opinion or feedback. On the contrary, someone with high external self-awareness and low internal self-awareness is primed to be a people-pleaser, focusing more on how they're perceived by others than understanding what's going on inside.

The goal of self-awareness is to balance internal and external self-awareness. How you see yourself should be the same as how you are seen by others. When the two sides match, you can target areas for improvement and change how you interact with yourself and with others.

Being able to master both sides of self-awareness is crucial for future leaders as they develop emotional intelligence.

CHAPTER TWO
THE IMPORTANCE OF
SELF-AWARENESS

Self-awareness (sometimes also referred to as self-knowledge or introspection) is about understanding your own needs, desires, failings, habits, and everything else that makes you the unique individual that you are. The more you know about yourself, the better you are at adapting to life's changes. When we have a better understanding of ourselves, we can experience ourselves as unique and separate individuals. This empowers us to make changes and build on our areas of strength, as well as identify areas where we would like to make improvements. Self-awareness is often the first step to setting goals.

It's impossible to better yourself or improve any aspect of your life without self-awareness. Without a starting point, how can you measure how far you've come or how far you still need to go?

Perhaps that's why so many of us cling to those distractions that we examined earlier. If you stay too busy to acknowledge your weaknesses, then you have no reason to work toward improvement. You can carry on and continue to ignore your deeply-rooted issues, fears, and feelings because hey, you've gotten this far and it's not that terrible yet. Or is it? Becoming more self-aware can help you to proactively manage your thoughts, emotions, and behaviors, rather than allowing them to manage you.

Self-awareness is the first step to setting goals. If you're self-aware enough to know your strengths and weaknesses, you'll know which goals you need to set and the strategies that will help you achieve them.

Without self-awareness, it is possible to imagine that everyone else has the same problems as you do. The reverse of the situation is also possible. In this situation, problems can be projected onto others. Being self-aware can enable one to mark their ego boundaries, and successfully discriminate between what belongs to someone else and what belongs to you. Secondly, self-awareness enables us to make conscious use of the self. That's what enables your life coach to deliver change behavior results with their client's well-being.

Being aware of yourself helps in identifying what your stressors are, so you can utilize the information to build effective coping mechanisms.

Being self-aware can help you relate well with people and increase your ability to achieve your goals. These are not the only benefits of self-awareness. Here are some more reasons why it is important to be self-aware.

1. Increases your social abilities

Human beings are social beings who thrive on relationships. Self-aware people are very successful when creating relationships. This is because they can realize exactly what they want in each person they meet. That certainty comes from knowing one's own abilities and challenges. Self-awareness also promotes emotional intelligence. Emotional intelligence helps us relate to the feelings of other people. Lacking this skill can leave us in conflict with others. The best way to improve your level of emotional intelligence is by learning your emotional patterns.

2. Promotes versatility and open-mindedness

Knowing yourself can be very crucial to affecting the approach that you have on issues. Self-awareness in itself is the ability to actively seek to listen to the body and mind to know your natural response to change. This consciousness can thus help you have a clear focus when dealing with issues. You are also able to accept opinions, feedback, and criticism from other people without being subjective. Ultimately, you can have multiple solutions to a single problem.

3. Promotes productivity

Self-aware people are fast thinkers. They understand themselves and can focus on the challenges of the day without hindrances. Without understanding yourself, there is a big challenge where you are held back by uncertainty. This results in time wastage caused by pondering over many different courses of action even when a swift decision is needed.

4. Improves leadership skills

One of the most important attributes of a good leader is swift decision-making. A leader should also be impartial and confident. All these are things that we gain by becoming self-aware. Knowing yourself removes internal fear and you can focus on important matters.

5. Promotes Overall Objectivity

Being self-aware promotes objectivity. Self-aware people are also self-confident. This means that they can easily make decisions without being clouded by poor judgment.

6. You'll have a better understanding of what affects your beliefs

We all have things we believe about ourselves, others, and how the world works. Religious and political beliefs are just two examples. These beliefs aren't developed spontaneously. They're influenced by factors like your upbringing and other life experiences. Self-aware people have a deeper understanding of where beliefs come from. This can make their beliefs stronger or trigger the development of new beliefs. As an example, most people have biases that can negatively affect others. A self-aware person is equipped to take a closer look at a bias and realize that it isn't a fact written in stone. This gives them space to change.

7. Improves critical thinking skills

Critical thinking is the ability to process and analyze information from an objective perspective. This is a very useful skill in many scenarios, whether personal or professional. When you're self-aware, you're able to identify the subjective parts of yourself – like your feelings and opinions – and do your best to not let them play too big of a role in your critical thinking.

8. Improves decision-making

Many skills go into making a good decision, and when you're self-aware, you already have many of those skills. Self-aware people are familiar with analyzing because they analyze their thoughts and feelings. They're also familiar with critical thinking, which is an important part of making a good decision. Knowing your strengths and weaknesses is also very helpful as it guides you to a decision that fits you best.

Better relationships. It's difficult to ask for what you want and need in a relationship—or set healthy boundaries—when you're not very clear about it yourself. For example, how well do you know your values? Often the best way to improve any relationship is by trying to become more you, more self-aware.

9. Calmer moods

How you consistently feel emotionally depends on how you think. If you have a habit of chronic worry, for example, you're very likely to feel anxious all the time. But when you improve your self-awareness, you learn to understand the relationship between your thinking and your moods. This makes it much easier to regulate your emotions effectively and balance your moods.

10. Clearer thinking and better decision-making

Poor decision-making often comes from muddled thinking and unchecked emotional reactions. When you become more aware of your habits, thoughts and feelings, you can more easily distinguish between short-term impulses or desires and long-term values and goals.

11. Increased productivity

The most common cause of procrastination and poor productivity isn't a lack of effort or commitment. It's interference from ourselves. When we struggle to get to work, it's usually because on some level our thoughts, emotions, or habits are getting in the way. Self-awareness can help eliminate many of these hidden obstacles to productivity.

12. You'll have more empathy

The benefits of self-awareness don't stop with you. Understanding yourself better translates into understanding others better. You become aware that everyone's feelings and beliefs come from their experiences. You're also a better listener, which is essential to fostering empathy. Considering that self-awareness is about understanding emotions, it makes sense that the understanding extends to others.

CHAPTER THREE
ELEMENTS AND QUALITIES OF SELF-AWARENESS

ELEMENTS OF SELF-AWARENESS

Have you ever wondered why you feel the way you do? Being able to recognize and understand your emotions can be the deciding factor in your successes or failures. Surprisingly, many people are not self-aware and their performance and communication suffer.

1. Self-Confidence

Self-awareness starts with self-confidence. When someone is self-confident, they have a positive outlook on life and will show compassion. This is important because if you constantly beat yourself up over your weaknesses, you are less likely, to be honest with yourself. Honesty and compassion with yourself are a must for developing self-awareness.

Your self-confidence is your perception of yourself. Your perceptions come from your personal experiences, what you expect from yourself in the future, and what you believe your abilities are. If your self-confidence is healthy, you are more likely to take on challenges, achieve goals you've set for yourself, and live more positively overall.

Explore your self-confidence and if you don't believe it's healthy, make an effort to change how you perceive yourself. This may be easier for some people and much harder for others — but it is possible.

2. Thoughts

Our thoughts are tied to our emotions, so when we try to become more aware of our emotions, we must first understand our thoughts and thought processes. Throughout the day, take note of what you say about yourself, how you talk about yourself, and what you say about situations you encounter.

If you notice your thoughts are more negative, practice mindfulness to discover why your thoughts are that way. Then, after reflecting, try to have more positive thoughts or thought processes. You might have to force it — you might not even believe it! But over time, it will influence your thoughts to be more positive.

3. Feelings

How do you feel when you say things about yourself? What about when other people say things about you? Feelings can lie, so no matter what your feelings are, you must identify which are associated with your thoughts and experiences.

Once you can identify those feelings, keep track of them and see if there are any patterns. Notice yourself starting down a negative pattern? Take steps to avoid continuing to go down with it.

4. Body

Sometimes when we're thinking, it comes with a physical response that other people may or may not notice! The next time you feel a physical response to an emotion, take a couple of minutes to think where in your body you feel the response. Do the feelings present in your facial expressions, heart rate, voice, or somewhere else? Is this the kind of physical response you want?

5. Emotions

Emotions are the most powerful factor in how we interact with others. People with higher levels of emotional intelligence can recognize and accept their varying emotional states. Knowing what emotional state you're in can go a long way toward enhancing your professional and personal relationships!

If you fail to recognize these responses, you will find it difficult to process your emotions and move past them. By effectively managing these elements, you will be able to control emotional outbursts and work toward a much more effective communication and an overall healthier, happier demeanor.

QUALITIES OF SELF-AWARENESS

The highest work you'll do in life is not in an office or occupation but within yourself. I don't do this internal research to understand my position in the world or to compare myself to others. I do it because I find knowledge and self-development to be incredibly enriching.

Unlike most things in life, your self-awareness never stops growing until your life is over. As you age, you come to understand life to a deeper degree as your own mortality sets in, and you walk closer to your terrestrial sunset.

The beauty of evolving internally is that it transcends class, money, career, and station in life. Everyone and anyone can become more evolved and aware. Everyone is given the opportunity at birth to do so, which is extraordinarily beautiful and such a gift.

One thing you should understand is you don't have to spend your time in a monastery sitting cross-legged to become more self-aware. All you have to do is want to be more self-aware and that is when your help begins. Think about the below five characteristics listed and assess how self-aware you might be.

1. Humility

Perhaps there is nothing more beautiful or powerful than a humble person.

Every amazing thing about you (and believe me there are many) is observable by those around you —it's not lost, maybe a little hidden. So when you practice humility in the world, your beautiful qualities are amplified to those around you.

When you practice humility, you tell people around you, "here, take my light and find your path today." What you're doing is the epitome of selflessness and shows how truly confident you are as a person. You are giving rather than receiving, and you are highlighting others instead of yourself.

I can't think of a more powerful way to exist in the world than to put others in front of yourself. So, let them have the win. Give the compliment. Pay for their drink at Starbucks. Give up your seat. Offer your help.

2. Discipline

The distance between two points in life is determined by your discipline to get there. The time it takes for you to do anything in life is all about how focused you are on the outcome. You can finish college in three years if you want to — but you make choices that keep you from graduation.

Professional athlete's are in their position because they put effort into the discipline it took to get there. Lindsey Vonn was the last skier on the little mountain she grew up on in Wisconsin — every night. She skied 12–14 hours a day; now, she's considered the best skier of all time. Discipline.

You might wonder, "what does that have to do with self-awareness?" I'll tell you! Someone with great discipline has immense power of the mind. Staying hyper-focused on the task at hand takes control of one's body and mind. It also takes tremendous belief in your abilities to succeed at that moment. Doing all of this requires a great deal of self-awareness into who you are and what you're made of internally.

3. Gratitude

Gratitude turns what we have into enough.

When you live with gratitude, life responds to you in full. Why? Because what you are saying is, "thank you, I have what I need; I am happy where I exist." When you commit to that train of thought, you are giving power to what is possible. You are also, unknowingly perhaps, opening up to accepting more — of what you want. You see, you are never given more than you are thankful for in life — even if it doesn't always feel that way. But unless you accept what is in this moment, acknowledge it and be grateful for it? How will you handle more? If you don't know where you've been, you can't see where you're going.

So instead of focusing on more, focus on the station where you are today with gratitude. See its lessons and linings and, then once it feels good, ask for more.

4. Integrity

Integrity is the ability to persist with one's beliefs through the headwinds of life.

We are all fabric of the human fray, becoming unraveled, independent strands as we age. It's in that unraveling away from humanity where we design our brand of integrity. Through our life, we gather the meaning of right and wrong. We experience others, and through the lens of each encounter, we grow into the beings we are meant to become. Unknowingly through our experiences, we sharpen our morals and beliefs throughout our lives.

It's through this process of learning — growing — breaking, that we either hold onto our integrity or we lose it bit by bit. The interesting thing about integrity is that we are all tested with this at some point.

Each of us will have the opportunity to show ourselves what our moral fabric is made of. When we are aware enough and strong enough in our beliefs, that fabric is chain-mail.

5. Passion

Passion is love.

When you live your passion, you are living your truth as your highest self, made in the image and likeness of our creator God. Often we think that our passion has to be this extraordinary station in life we must attain at all costs. Guess what? Let that notion go because this comes from a place of comparison, which is robbing you of your happiness.

You are a unique and ever-changing person who is continually shifting and growing. Your passions will change as you go through the phases of your life

None of the aforementioned five characteristics are beyond any of us. This isn't an exclusive club that comes with a black card and diamond logo. You, me, and everyone we know can become higher-functioning self-aware human beings.

If you want to start practicing the characteristics listed, take a step back away from your life, just for a few minutes. Get a piece of paper out and jot down your thoughts on each one. How am I humble? What do I practice discipline with? What is my passion? What does integrity mean to me? What am I grateful for?

Remember, the rate at which you evolve your self-awareness is up to you. Life isn't a dress rehearsal, and every day is a chance to explore the borders of your internal landscape. How far those borders grow comes down to how much broader you hope to make your self-awareness footprint.

CHAPTER FOUR
HOW SELF-AWARE ARE YOU?

What have you done to understand how others perceive you? Do you understand your limitations and develop them? Try these strategies to develop your self-awareness. Get your journal and...

Look inside yourself:

- What do you do well?

- What do you like to do?

- What do you not like to do?

- What do you repeat regularly because it works, or not?

- How do you describe yourself?

- What do you stand for?

- Do you have a development plan?

Look outside yourself:

- Look at your client or social roster - what are they like?

- To what types of groups or organizations do you belong?

- What does your daily routine look like?

- What have you accomplished in the last 3 years?

- Who is on your team?

Ask others:

- If you could see a pattern in my life what would it be?

- If you could change one thing about me, what would it be?

- Describe me and my brand.

In all of the above research, honesty and clarity are key. You need to be honest with yourself and others need to trust that you will accept their information in the spirit in which it is intended - answering the questions you are asking to build your self-awareness and develop steps to become the person and leader you want to be.

At the end of your personal assessment and research, you will want to take time to see where opposites or similarities lie in the responses. Use this information to create a personal development plan for yourself. A personal development plan can be built as a goal sheet with clear action points that will help improve the skills you would like to develop. Revisiting this plan quarterly to note your progress and make adjustments will help you reach your goals. Try hiring a coach for a year or more and watch the growth increase in quality and speed.

When you discover things that are great about yourself, you need to take action to leverage those strengths so they help build your developmental areas into stronger components of your leadership. Not easy, but a very valuable exercise.

SIGNS YOU ARE MORE SELF-AWARE THAN YOU MAY THINK

Who am I? "I'm ambitious." "I'm curious." "I'm goal-oriented." "I'm strong-willed." "I'm independent." "I'm a learner." "I'm an achiever".

Not a single person has an exact answer to this question. However, if something close to these answers crossed your mind, congratulations, you're more self-aware than you may think!

But what does it mean to be self-aware?

Many people think that self-awareness is this grandiose skill that only super-smart people understand. This is far from true. If you have fallen victim to this type of thinking, I want to share some signs that you may be more self-aware than you think you are.

1. You think about your thought processes.

Thinking is a part of our everyday lives. We wake up and think about simple things, such as making breakfast. Sometimes we're faced with serious problems and think about ways to deal with them. But how often do you think about how much you think?

In psychology, psychologist know the process of "metacognition." In simple words, it's thinking about what you are thinking about. If this process is familiar to you, you probably won't be surprised by discovering that metacognition helps you become more self-aware.

Do you have a deep understanding of your thoughts? Do you try to criticize popular opinions instead of accepting them unconditionally? If the answer is yes, then you can use your thoughts to move forward and become more self-aware.

2. You're Unapologetically Yourself.

If you aren't afraid to speak your truth, for fear that others won't accept you for who you are, chances are you have a high level of self-awareness.

Self-aware people live from a place of integrity. They are unapologetically themselves, in the sense that they don't allow the noise of other's judgments to veer them off track. In other words, they know how to stay in their lane.

3. You're The Master of Your Emotions.

When life doesn't go your way, self-aware people don't react and throw in the towel. They understand that irrational behaviors only make you spiral into a negative hole. Hence, they stop and think before they respond to challenges.

They know that if they don't master their emotions, their emotions will master them. By becoming aware of their emotions, they can maintain a sense of clarity and peace of mind, no matter what is going on in their environment.

4. You Listen to Yourself.

Self-aware individuals pride themselves on their ability to pay attention and tune into what is happening inside of them. Your intuition rarely ever lies.

I have yet to meet anyone who has said to me, "My gut is a liar." Self-aware people listen to what their gut tells them. When something doesn't feel right, it probably isn't. By trusting the messages or feelings that they are receiving, self-aware people are better able to make decisions that positively influence their lives. Self-aware people have a better relationship with the Holy Spirit as they can better accept His presence in their life.

5. You're very honest about what you love, what you hate, and everything else in between.

You have strong opinions on certain things and aren't afraid to share them (with tact and only when it's appropriate, of course). You don't pretend to have strong opinions on things you generally have a neutral stance on. You also don't try to force yourself to love something you hate or hate something you love.

6. You tend to overanalyze the way you come across to other people, from every single angle possible.

You don't want to talk too much or too little. You think about what you want to say and carefully phrase it in a way that benefits you and the people you're speaking to. You want to be considerate of other peoples time. You're polite and aren't too keen on burning bridges or saying things out of impulse. You know when to stop yourself before getting too vulnerable. You also use your overly self-conscious tendencies for good and make sure you're well-groomed and presentable. You understand the power of presenting yourself in a manner that is neither fake nor inconsiderate.

7. You've Got Strong Boundaries.

Self-aware people don't let others walk all over them. They know that they can't be all things for all people, which is why they establish strong boundaries with others. Setting a boundary is the ability to recognize the need for a healthy separation between your thoughts and feelings and the thoughts and feelings of others. By taking care of your emotional needs first, self-aware people are better able to take care of themselves.

8. You don't expect life to give you special privileges.

You acknowledge that fulfillment isn't about making the world see you as more significant or nobler than everyone else and that many constraints and barriers can hinder you, but you work with what you have instead of complaining about how unfair life is. You don't expect to be given more than what you put in.

9. You don't get defensive when people criticize you.

You understand that while people's opinions of you don't define who you are, you take the time to listen and consider that you might have a few unresolved issues that only you can take the time to find solutions for. You know that reacting defensively is a warning sign of insecurity.

10. You accept that there's so much that you don't know.

People who have high levels of self-awareness easily accept the fact that they don't know everything. And we can't know everything.

"The more you know, the more you realize you don't know." That's what Aristotle said.

Consider the diversity of our world. Someone living in Central Europe may be the most competent person in their literature class, but at the same time, he or she has no idea what is going on in the schools of the far east.

That's normal. Not knowing things is typical. That's why we should accept that there's so much that we don't know. Pretending to know everything just doesn't work. And it's not useful either. But accepting that you don't know a lot of things will help you focus on your goals and find out what is something you don't know but want to learn

11. You can look at things from different perspectives and accept other's opinions.

If I ask you whether you consider others opinions while making a mistake, you're likely to agree. That's off of the biases that affect our decision-making process. In reality, looking at things from other' perspectives isn't easy. But it's possible!

I'm not saying that you should accept others' opinions and change your beliefs based on how others think. Instead, trusting your beliefs is what makes people self-aware, but only if you respect others' opinions too.

12. You don't avoid making hard decisions.

Do you procrastinate about making decisions? Do you avoid taking risks even when you feel that they will help you grow? Then it's time to move on.

Realizing your strengths and weaknesses is part of self-awareness. Sometimes it's important to make hard decisions and maybe even fail. Why? Because successful people acknowledge that taking risks is a part of self-development.

Think about it. Do you try to assess your thoughts and feelings objectively if you chronically avoid making difficult decisions?

SELF-AWARENESS ASSESSMENT

The questions for self-awareness, along with a brief description of their meaning and importance, are listed below.

1. Can you name the behaviors that you are doing at all times?

   a) Yes, I'm always intentional with my behaviors and can name what I'm taking part in at all times.

   b) Occassionally, I'm aware of what I'm doing, although, at times, I get caught up in something or don't realize what I'm doing.

   c) No, I rarely am aware of what my body or mind is doing.

While it might seem obvious, it can be challenging to recognize our behaviors. Statistics say that every day, we make over 2,000 decisions per hour. Because this number is so high, our brain usually takes over and acts without us being conscious of it. Our emotional brain has more power than our thinking brain does. All of these unconscious decisions decrease our self-awareness. We also default to our typical routines and patterns without consciously identifying the shift.

2. Can you name the emotions that you are feeling at all times?

> a) Yes, I can always identify and name the emotion I'm feeling at any given moment.

> b) Occassionally, I'm aware of what emotion I'm feeling. However, it takes me a few moments to recognize it, and strong emotions sometimes catch me off-guard.

> c) No, I rarely think about what emotion I'm feeling. I just feel something and act accordingly.

Emotional intelligence is perhaps the foundation of all self-awareness, but it's not easy. Humans are wired to seek pleasure and avoid pain. Our amygdala sparks emotions deep within us. These driving emotions get in the way of our rational thinking. The more self-aware you are of your emotions, the better you can control them.

3. Can you identify what causes a shift to negative emotions?

> a) Yes, I can always identify what causes me to shift to negative emotions, whether it be an event, person, or recurring trigger.

> b) Sometimes. I can usually identify what caused a shift in emotions, although it takes a little while for me to catch on.

> c) No, I rarely know what specifically causes me to shift to negative emotions. All of a sudden, I'm no longer happy and I don't know why.

I know it's difficult to believe, but we don't just "switch" to negative emotions for no apparent reason. There's always something that causes this shift. The problem is that we don't always know what this "something" is (generally because it's hard enough just to name our negative emotions in the first place). After taking this free self-awareness assessment, try to consciously recognize when you shift into a bad mood and what might have caused it.

4. Can you name the emotional patterns you experience the most?

   a) Yes, I can list my standard emotional patterns right now, including what they are, what causes them, and what effect they have on my life.

   b) Sometimes, I know what I tend to do, but its not always consistent or recognizable.

   c) No, I have no idea what emotional patterns I repeat. I have emotions, but I can't name any trends with when or why they happen.

If emotions are difficult to identify, emotional patterns can be even trickier. We all fall into emotional patterns, both negative and positive, that repeat themselves in our lives. Once you're self-aware of these patterns, you can begin to improve your negative patterns and construct your positive ones.

5. Can you name your deepest fear triggers?

   a) Yes, I'm self-aware of my deepest fears and what triggers these fears in my everyday life. I understand how pervasive these fears are in my thoughts and actions.

   b) Somewhat. I can tell you what I'm most scared of, but I don't fully know how it affects my life and daily actions.

   c) No, I have no idea what a fear trigger even is or if I have one.

One of the strongest human motivators is the emotion of fear. Starting in our history, fear helped us survive from potential threats. In today's age fear still drives us, even when we are not in imminent danger. Additionally, we've all developed our deep-rooted fears. By increasing your self-awareness of what causes your fear, you can better manage your emotional reactions when it gets triggered.

6. Can you name your deepest shame triggers?

    a) Yes, I know the things that give me the most shame and what triggers this shame in my everyday life. I understand how pervasive this shame is in my thoughts and actions.

    b) Somewhat. I can tell you what I'm most ashamed of, but I don't fully know how it affects my life and daily actions.

    c) No, I have no idea what a shame trigger even is or if I have one.

The other powerful motivating emotion is shame. We're not self-aware of how shame, and the avoidance of shame, drive our thinking and behaviors. To limit the effect that shame has, we need to develop greater self-awareness of what triggers our shame the most.

7. Can you name the principles and values you believe in the most?

    a) Yes, I can list my guiding principles and core values right now. I know how to distinguish between what I care about and the outside influence of others.

    b) Somewhat. I can name a few principles and qualities that are most important to me, but I haven't given this list a lot of thought.

    c) No, I have no idea what values I believe in the most.

Self-awareness extends beyond identifying our emotions (although being self-aware of our emotions is the foundation). Understanding our principles and core values is a crucial component of self-awareness. To be happy, you must discover what core values you want to guide your life.

8. How much do you consider these principles when making decisions?

a) A lot. Not only do I know what these principles are, but I design my life and decision-making around them. They give clarity to my decisions.

b) Somewhat. I know what my principles are but don't know when they come into effect in my life.

c) Not at all. I live my life without ever giving a thought to any principles.

Naming your core values is the first step. The second step includes using these principles to guide your life and decision-making. To be self-aware, you must understand how to orient your decision-making around your core values. Only with this self-awareness can you give your life the direction you want.

9. Can you name the passions that you have and which passions cause you to lose track of time while doing them?

a) Yes, I know what I'm passionate about and why they give me joy.

b) Somewhat. I can list things that I enjoy doing, although I wouldn't necessarily call them passions.

c) No, I don't have any clear passions.

Many of us have a false idea of what passion and purpose should look like. Passions do not need to consume your life. Instead, passions are the things that you do that give you joy and energy. We all have passions; it merely takes some self-awareness to identify them and prioritize them in your life.

10. Can you state a list of goals and ambitions you have for yourself?

a) Yes, I can state a list of goals right now that include both short-term and long-term goals. I understand what I want out of life and can express these ambitions.

b) Somewhat. I have a few goals and ambitions, although they might not be the most defined.

c) No, I don't have any driving goals or ambitions in my life.

Humans are wired for self-growth. This growth is difficult to achieve, if you're not self-aware of what you should be growing toward. Self-improvement needs to start with clear goals, and it takes a level of self-awareness to be able to state these goals and pursue them

11. Can you describe the environment you thrive in the most?

a) Yes, I can describe the ideal environment that I need to be happy and be successful, including the pace, energy, and structure that I thrive in.

b) Somewhat. I know certain things that I would want, but I can't fully describe the exact environment that I thrive in.

It's easy to only look inward when we think of self-awareness. However, real self-awareness also requires us to look outward. The more self-aware you are about your environment and how it affects you, the more you can design your life in a way that brings purpose to your life.

12. Can you identify a list of personal strengths and how they manifest themselves in your life?

a) Yes, I can list all of my strengths right now, as well as where they fit into my life and how I use them to find success.

b) Somewhat. I mostly know what I'm good at, although I couldn't tell you exactly how I incorporate these strengths into my life.

c) No.

There's a reason why, there are a lot of strength-finding assessment. Being self-aware of your strengths, and how they manifest themselves in your life, is crucial to being successful in life.

13. Can you identify a list of shortcomings and how they manifest themselves in your life?

    a) Yes, I can list all of my shortcomings right now, as well as how they affect my life and what I need to do to overcome them.

    b) Somewhat. I mostly know what my weaknesses are, although I don't have an exact list.

    c) No, I might even try to avoid them, and I don't know how they hold me back.

As fun as it might be to discover our strengths, it might be unpleasant to look for our shortcomings. However, understanding our limitations is 100% necessary to be successful. Possessing the self-awareness of these limitations can help us design our life in a way that is realistic and effective.

14. Can you describe your typical reaction to new information, whether it be positive or negative?

    a) Yes, I can tell you right now how I usually react to new information. I understand my natural tendencies with both what emotions I feel and what impulses I have.

    b) Somewhat. I can generally describe how I react to positive and negative news, but I'm not fully aware of my emotions and thoughts.

    c) No, I just react at the moment and don't know of any patterns.

We don't often think about a "typical" reaction, because every new piece of information feels new. However, if you do think about it, you can become self-aware of your reactions and how they repeat themselves. By doing so, you can work to downplay the negative reactions and build on your positive ones.

15. Can you name what you need in your relationships to feel fulfilled?

   a) Yes, I can name exactly what I need in my life in my relationships to create a sense of belonging and feel fulfilled. Additionally, I'm able to express these needs.

   b) Somewhat. I know what I need from others, although I might not know specifically what I need from each person or in different situations.

   c) No, I don't know what I need from my relationships to feel fulfilled.

We often think of relationships in terms of two people, but this narrow perspective is doing more harm than good. You must be self-aware of what you need to build meaningful relationships in your life. Trust me – self-awareness will immediately improve your relationships.

SCORING THIS SELF-AWARENESS ASSESSMENT

For clear results, you should consider what questions you answered: "b's" and "c's" for. For any question you answered "b" for, how can you bring greater clarity into your life in this area? For your "c" answers, it's time to start the journey of self. I'd suggest you dive into the topic and be intentional with questioning yourself to find the answers you're looking for. Again, you might want to consider hiring a life coach. You are too important to ignore another day or year.

Taking this self-awareness assessment and viewing your results is step one in improving your self-awareness. You can see how self-aware you are, and you can identify where you might be lacking self-awareness in your life.

However, step two requires a bit more action. Self-awareness is not something you can achieve through one simple assessment or activity. It takes patience and purposeful practice. Unfortunately, most of us are going about self-awareness all wrong.

CHAPTER FIVE
HABITS OF PEOPLE WITH HIGH SELF-AWARENESS

Self-awareness is, as the name implies, the ability to look at oneself. What is one looking at? Usually, emotional and thought processes, including beliefs, motivation, strengths, and weaknesses. Self-awareness also permits one to look at how others perceive them.

The ability to monitor ourselves from moment to moment is the key to understanding who we are and our relative place in the world. Moreover, self-awareness is an essential component of happiness and wellbeing.

"Most people do not listen with the intent to understand; they listen with the intent to reply." ~ Stephen Covey

Practice active listening

The reality is that when most of us listen to someone, we're thinking about our reply before the individual finishes. Or, worse, there's something that we're just so itching to say that we completely interrupt the person.

Here's another thing: we can't possibly build self-awareness if we don't take an interest in what others have to say. We can't build self-awareness if we don't practice active listening. It's an essential skill to cultivate for this and many other reasons.

We should want to cultivate active listening. Why? Because it helps us to empathize, understand, obtain information, learn, and even enjoy ourselves.

Active listening means to "concentrate, understand, respond, and then remember what is being said." Let's look at each one of these.

Concentrate: You must direct and hold your attention to what's being said.

Understand: If you concentrated well through the conversation, you should have a good understanding of it. However, you may still have questions. If so, ask them.

Respond: If you followed the concentrate and understand, elements you are well-equipped to respond.

Remember: If you've engaged wholly in active listening throughout the conversation, recall shouldn't be too much trouble.

Get curious about how your mind works

Self-awareness requires paying attention to what's going on between our ears. We must understand how our brains work before any type of tinkering to awareness can happen.

As such, highly self-aware person knows the inner workings of their minds. They know how it acts and reacts, as well as its strengths and weaknesses. Indeed, this is the quintessential function of self-awareness.

How to do this?

First, you must be completely honest with yourself. Our ego has an entrenched and often subtle defense mechanisms that require bypassing. We accomplish this by objectively observing ourselves.

Here's a basic framework for mind investigation:

What are my predominant mental and emotional states? Which ones are positive? Negative?

How do I feel when accomplishing something? How can I get into that state of mind?

What things do I do that make me feel better? Worse? How can I get into those states where I feel better?

Solicit feedback – and welcome it all

One sign of outstanding self-awareness is seeking feedback. The problem: so many of us are far too sensitive, proud, or fearful, to willingly ask someone for their honest assessment. We're scared of what they might say.

The thing is that feedback is critical in any endeavor, including the betterment of our self-awareness

Do you remember that jittery feeling in school before getting back test results? How about right before a job evaluation? Of course, you do! That's fearfulness (some call it anxiety, but that's another word for fear.)

It may be comforting to know that we all – to a greater or lesser degree – fear the feedback of others. But that doesn't stop the self-aware from seeking it out.

There's also the fact that the person whom you're seeking feedback from will admire both your courageousness and willingness to improve. Imagine what that shift in perspective can do for you, both personally and professionally!

Be reflective and thoughtful towards yourself and others

You can't be self-aware if you're not attentive. The ability to look at yourself – your feelings and behaviors– is an essential element of self-awareness.

It's not only about being reflective and thoughtful towards yourself. It's also about extending these qualities to others. You do this mostly through how you communicate, interact with, and respond to people.

Here's an example, you receive a harshly-worded, borderline-inappropriate email from a client about your job performance.

You can feel yourself become angry, and your thinking clouded. At the moment, there's nothing you want to do more than give a piece of your mind to the ungrateful urchin that is your customer. Do you follow through?

Notice that, with a couple of tweaks, the above scenario applies to pretty much any situation, anywhere. Maybe it's your kids, your spouse, your co-workers. Perhaps it's not an email, but a text message, a passing conversation, or a slight remark. Instead of critiquing professional understanding, it's the scrutinization of your social etiquette.

Regardless of the context, the premise is the same: you're being told something that you don't want to hear. Now, instead of blowing a fuse, do the hard thing and reflect on the situation.

Here are a few questions to ask yourself:

- Is the underlying message (minus the perceived aggression, vitriol, etcetera) in any way justifiable?

- Is this how the person feels about me?

- Have I done anything – intentional or unintentional – that may have led, or even contributed, to this encounter?

While this is a hard thing to do, asking yourself these questions – and taking the appropriate actions – will contribute to your personal development in ways unimaginable.

Don't "do" self-awareness, "be" self-aware

This point is critical if a bit subtle. In the beginning phases of any endeavor there is some effort involved. This includes the practice of self-awareness. There's a specific "doing" of self-awareness that happens as one acclimates to "being" self-aware.

It's important to know that, after a certain point, there's no conscious "doing" of self-awareness. As long as there's continuous exertion, the skill of self-awareness continues to develop. More importantly, it demonstrates that there's critical work to be done.

Self-aware people are often, ironically, less aware of their innate awareness.

They're kind instead of nice

The word "nice" has roots in the following:

- Foolish

- Stupid

- Senseless

- Careless

- Clumsy

- Weak

- Poor

- Needy

- Ignorant

- Unaware

The word "kind" has roots in the following:

- Deliberately doing good to others

- Innate

- Natural

- Compassionate

- Loving

- Full of tenderness

I know which list I prefer, and I know which list I prefer to practice on myself.

Poor beliefs can be changed

I want you to think about your most important belief. One that guides your life. One that you lean on when you need something to lean on.

I want you to remove it from your head. I want you to hold it in your hand. I want you to close that hand.

Now, open that hand. What's in that hand?

Your belief, right?

Nope.

There's nothing in your hand.

Your most important belief, the belief that guides you, the belief you lean on... it's not real but yet it can guide your life.

So... what about poor beliefs or more direct, beliefs passed down to you that are guiding your life and they aren't good for you. Why does it seem so hard to let go of them sometimes? Why does it seem so hard to change? Why wouldn't we just let go and take on different beliefs all the time, depending on what we need?

What about the beliefs that aren't useful to you? What's stopping you from letting them go? A belief that you need them?

Self-aware people know they need certainty and uncertainty

Humans need certainty and uncertainty. This is a fact.

Too much certainty = boredom.

Too much uncertainty = anxiety.

It's good to be certain about your health, about your relationships, about your finances.

But imagine being certain about every single minute of every single day of your entire life. How boring would that be? How depressing would that be?

We need both.

You are more than their thoughts

You're the one who experiences your thoughts. You're the one who hears them. You're the one who can control them.

So... you must be something else. Something different. Something more.

That means that you're not required to do whatever your thoughts wish for you to do. You don't have to obey them. They're not in charge -- you are. The real you.

It's like this quote from Michael A. Singer, author of The Surrender Experiment and The Untethered Soul:

"The day you decide you are more interested in being aware of your thoughts than you are in the thoughts themselves -- that is the day you will find your way out."

Know you're more than your feelings

Same thing as being more than your thoughts. Your feelings aren't there to tell you how to act, and they're not there to tell you whether or not to act at all. They're there to tell you what's important to you.

I have another quote for you, this time from Victor Frankl, author of Man's Search For Meaning:

"Between stimulus and response, there is a space. In that space is our power to choose our response."

They never waste a perfectly good mistake.

I learned this from Michael Houlihan and Bonnie Harvey, the entrepreneurs behind one of the biggest wine brands in the world -- Barefoot Wine. They say that there's no excuse for wasting a perfectly good mistake because every mistake is beautiful. After all, now you've got the opportunity to never make the same mistake again.

Never making the same mistake again is real self-awareness. It's funny though -- it's another one of those things that people say is "hard." It's "hard" to admit to your own mistakes. But... is it? Because what's the alternative? Making the same mistake over and over and over and never moving forward and never becoming who you know you could be? That's hard to me!

Does that sound "easier"?

Know that your opinion of who you are is more important than
     anyone else's opinion of who you are

If other people's opinions of you are more important to you than your own... then how can you expect to live a life that's true to you? How can you expect to ever stop worrying about what other people think of you? How will you ever feel free?

Do you think your opinion of someone else should be more important than that person's opinion of themselves? I doubt it! And yet... it's somehow okay for other people's opinions of you to be more important to you than your own?

Other people are allowed to be who they are, but you have to be who other people want you to be?

You are allowed to put yourself first

If I asked you to write down a list of the important people in your life, would you write your name?

If so, where would you write it? Right at the top? In the middle? At the bottom?

When I put other people above me is when I lived by their expectations instead of my own. It's when I wanted their approval, their permission, their support. It's not when I wanted it. It's when I needed it. Well, when I believed I needed it. And because I needed it... when I didn't get it, I didn't do the thing I wanted their permission to do.

That means I didn't get what I wanted to get. All I got was frustration, and annoyance, and unhappiness.

Because I didn't think it was ok to put myself first.

You have no control over other people so how can it be ok to put anybody else at the top of your list?

How can they be more important to you than you are?

It's less about "how to" and more about "what's stopping me?"

I get asked a lot of "how-to" questions.

How to stop procrastinating, how to stay motivated, how to get over my ex.

All of them have the same answer: figure out why you're doing it, and then stop doing it. And you probably won't even need to "stop" -- figuring out why is usually enough to stop.

But, of course, that's not the answer people want. They already know that answer. So they need more.

Asking "what's stopping me" questions can be scarier because they go deeper. "How to" questions are surface questions. They're easy to answer. But "what's stopping me" questions give answers like "because I'm scared" or "because I don't want to" or "because I don't know if I can."

Admitting to those, confronting those... that's self-awareness.

CHAPTER SIX
HOW TO IMPROVE YOUR SELF-AWARENESS

"Self-awareness is one of the rarest of human commodities. I don't mean self-consciousness where you're limiting and evaluating yourself. I mean being aware of your patterns."

– Tony Robbins

Before knowing anything else, you need to know yourself first. You need to know your weaknesses, strengths, beliefs, and desires in life. Keeping in touch with your emotions means, you have to be self-aware.

At its core, being self-aware means that you can understand why you feel the way you do and make decisions that honor your needs. This can include personal goals, boundaries, and relationships. Becoming self-aware is not something that individuals are always inherently born with, instead, it is a skill learned over time.

By being self-aware you can move through life in a way that honors your individual needs and emotions. Though this is a learned skill some people may find that they come to it more naturally than others. Having self-awareness means that you have a sharp realization of your personality, including your strengths and weaknesses, your thoughts and beliefs, your emotions, and your motivations.

If you are self-aware, it is easier for you to understand other people and detect how they perceive you in return. While you develop self-awareness, your thoughts and interpretations will begin to change. This change in mental state will also alter your emotions and increase your emotional intelligence, which is an important factor in achieving overall success.

Improving your self-awareness is the first step in the creation of your ideal future. It's the personal commitment to yourself that you are ready and willing to upgrade your current reality. Once you are more aware of your thoughts, emotions, and behaviors, you become empowered to make changes that serve your highest self.

Envision yourself

Visualize the best version of yourself. "Ideal selves reflect our hopes, dreams, aspirations, and speak to our skills, abilities, achievements, and accomplishments that we wish to attain." As you lean into your strengths to become the better version of yourself, you can use this idealized self to keep moving in the right direction and not be distracted by setbacks and other obstacles.

Ask the "what" questions

At the core of self-awareness is the ability to self-reflect. However, the Eurich group contends that most people are going about reflection in the wrong way. The trouble is, we ask ourselves the wrong questions. In our attempt to resolve internal conflict, we ask, "Why?" Yet theres no way to answer that question since we don't have access to our unconscious. Instead, we make up answers that may not be accurate.

The danger of the "why" question is that it sends us down the rabbit hole of our negative thoughts. We focus on our weaknesses and insecurities. Consider Amy, a new junior executive who has difficulty speaking up at meetings. She may explain her experience to herself by thinking, "I don't speak up at meetings because I fall too low in the corporate food chain. No one's going to listen to me."

Asking the "what question" puts us into the objective and open space of considering all the factors influencing a particular outcome. For example, instead of "Why don't I speak up at meetings?" we could ask:

- "What were the interpersonal dynamics in the room?"

- "What was I experiencing in my body at the time?"

- "What happened that caused me to go into my old story of not being good enough?"

- "What can I do to overcome my fear of speaking up?

This kind of introspection allows us to look at behaviors and beliefs for what they are. With self-awareness, we can examine old patterns and stories that do not serve us, and then we can move on. Asking the right questions empowers us to make different choices that bring different results.

For example, Amy decides to make a plan because now she understands that she has a chance at overcoming her problem.

She's going to find out more about the content and goals of an upcoming meeting to become more confident in how she can contribute.

- Rather than being consumed by imagining what others are thinking about her, she'll actively listen for cues to ask meaningful questions that move the conversation forward.

- With a heightened awareness of the cues her body is giving her signaling fear and anxiety, she'll name the emotion at the moment and choose not to be overwhelmed by it — one giant step to self-awareness.

Ask "What?" instead of "Why?"

When people assess their current state, emotions, and environment, they all too often ask, "Why?" Like, "Why am I feeling so sad? Why did my boss give me that feedback? Why isn't my project going the way I'd hoped?"

Here's why asking "Why?" is ineffective:

Research has shown, you don't have access to a lot of your unconscious thoughts, feelings, and motives. Odds are, you're wrong about why you act, do, or think certain things. For instance, you might hear harsh feedback from a boss, and rationale it's because you're not cut out for the job, or harp on your insecurities -- it's hard for you to unbiasedly evaluate your strengths and weaknesses and come to a correct conclusion.

Rather than asking "Why," highly self-aware people ask, "What?" "What" questions are more productive, and focus on objectives and future goals, rather than past mistakes.

For instance, let's say you're feeling frustrated at work. "Why am I feeling awful?" Will likely only leave you feeling more depressed, forcing you to ruminate on negatives. On the other hand, "What are the situations at work making me feel bad?" Guides you to recognizing factors outside your control that don't align with your passions or goals, and helps you strategize how to fix those situations.

Spend time with yourself

It's not easy to reflect on yourself when you've got the TV blaring, you're out to dinner with friends, or you're glued to your phone.

Give yourself the space and time necessary to self-reflect, by avoiding distractions. Try spending time reading, writing, meditating, or practicing other solo activities to connect with yourself.

Try to give yourself 30 quiet, distraction-free minutes a day.

Know your Strengths and Weaknesses

Knowing your strengths and coping with your weaknesses, will help you improve self-awareness. Each of us has strengths and weaknesses that compose who we are and this will help you shape how to reach your goals. Your weaknesses hold you back from achieving many great things while your strengths are something that comes very easily for you to take. You should take ownership of assessing yourself because it is for your personal development.

Use Your Brain

The amygdala, also called the primitive brain, was the first part of the brain to develop in humans. It functioned as a kind of radar signaling the need to run away or fight back. That part of the brain is skilled at anticipating danger and reacts before we can even name a negative emotion. Our heart races, our stomach tightens, and our neck muscles tense up.

Your body's reaction is a tripwire signaling the pre-frontal cortex to register or name a negative emotion. If you bring awareness to your physical state, you can, at the moment, recognize the emotion as it is happening. Becoming skillful at this rewires your brain.

Naming your feelings is critical in decision-making. When we let our feelings overwhelm us, we can make bad decisions with unintended consequences. Naming your emotions allows us to take a "third-person" perspective to stand back and more objectively evaluate what's going on.

Let's bring this home with an example. You, a self-aware person, are having a conversation with someone and receiving some negative feedback. Your heart starts to race, and you're feeling threatened. You say to yourself, "I feel like this person is attacking me." But, before you cry or go ballistic, you stop yourself and hear the person out. You discover that this person had at least one good point and start up a different conversation, one that is mutually satisfying and productive.

Ask others about their perception of you

Now that you've discovered that feedback doesn't have to be scary, ask other people how they perceive you in certain situations. Getting specific will help to give you the most concrete feedback. Get brave and ask them how they would like to see you behave.

Exercise: Pick out a scenario(s) you would like to receive feedback on and list them.

Make two columns:

Column A: How I see myself

Column B: How others see me

In Column A make a list of words to describe your attitude and behaviors at the time.

Then, ask your feedback partner to do the same and record those responses in Column B.

Look out for discrepancies. You may have some blind spots that need attending.

Write Things Down

Keep a journal, start a blog, send emails to yourself, scribble in a notebook—however, you do it, writing is a lot like meditating with an active brain component added in.

That's because writing has a way of forcing you to focus your mind and get clear about exactly what it is you're thinking and feeling (see a pattern here?).

As the author, Flannery O'Connor said, "I write because I don't know what I think until I read what I say."

You don't have to write beautifully or even all that well to get the benefits of this. The simple act of organizing your thoughts on paper is often enough to give you more clarity about your thoughts and feelings than keeping it all bottled up between your ears.

Develop Intuitive Decision-Making Skills

Intuition plays a significant role in developing your self-awareness. This can be the source of significant errors in the course of decision-making. Your intuition will help you navigate faster yet, this can also be misled if too many of your facts are wrong. Moreover, this will help you, even more, this is an effective way to feed your subconscious mind.

Practice Self-Discipline

In every area of your life, you need to practice self-discipline. It is a trait that provides you with the enduring focus necessary for you. If you want to control your desires and impulses to stay focused on what you think needs to get done to successfully achieve that goal, you need to practice self-discipline. This will also help you develop your potential and improve your awareness since self-discipline helps you form habits to attain your goals in life.

Take Psychometric Tests

While there are plenty of online tests, grab them as long as you can, because this might help you find out if you are an Analyst, Diplomat, Sentinel, or Explorer. I use www.16personalities.com. There are also, other best-known tests like Myers-Briggs and Predictive Index but all of these are aimed at serving as a data point towards greater self-awareness. Reflecting on trade-off questions helps test-takers better understand their true characters.

Practice mindfulness

Mindfulness is a practice. It helps you be aware of what's going on in your mind, body, and environment. Meditation is one of a few practices that you can insert into your daily life, and practicing mindfulness is a wonderful tool for developing greater self-control.

The road to self-awareness is a journey. The most self-aware people see themselves on a quest to mastery rather than at a particular destination. As you move forward in developing your self-awareness, ask yourself regularly, "How will you move toward the best version of yourself today?" You must focus with some degree of concentration on what you are thinking and feeling at a given moment. Then you must clarify those thoughts and feelings: where do they occur in your body, how exactly do they feel—warm/cold, tight/open, exciting/fear-inducing, etc.—are they fleeting or enduring, and so on.

Meditation, as I've already alluded to, is one such tool to help you practice being more mindful. But meditation as a practice by itself is not the goal. Again, it simply teaches you how to be more aware of what you're thinking and feeling, usually while you're sitting quietly without any external distractions (but meditation can technically be done in any environment).

The goal is to take the self-awareness skills you learn from meditation and apply them to your everyday life, being more focused with more clarity and more accepting of what is going on at any given moment.

Learning how to do mindfulness meditation is relatively simple.

Here is an excellent technique to get started:

    i. Find a place where you won't be disturbed. You may sit in a chair or on the floor. Be sure to keep your back and neck straight.

    ii. As you begin, try and stay focused on the present moment. Don't think about the past or the future.

    iii. Develop an awareness of the breath, and focus on the feeling of air moving in and out of your body as you breathe in and out. Notice your belly rising and falling, as the air enters your nostrils and leaves your mouth. Notice how each breath is a little different.

    iv. Notice every thought that comes and goes. You can even name your thoughts. If you are worried, acknowledge that and let it go. Don't ignore your thoughts, but make a note of them, using your breath as an anchor.

    v. If you have trouble staying focused on the present moment, bring your focus back to your breathing, and don't be too hard on yourself.

    vi. Strive for a minute or so initially and work your way up to longer periods.

Meditating on the scriptures

Meditating on your faith or the scriptures is a wonderful way to ground yourself. According to www.gospelcoalition.org "daydreaming lets your mind wander, whereas with meditation, you intentionally focus your thoughts on positive things."

Connecting with your faith, and the earth and bringing your focus into the present moment, is similar to mindfulness.

You will give your attention to a verse, phrase, word, song or teaching of scripture that you have chosen.

1. Find a comfortable chair or couch to sit in. I like to sit in front of a window with a peaceful view of a tree or flower garden. Sometimes I sit Indian-style in front of the window in the early hours of the morning to start my day off. I start with my eyes open, and then usually, I'm able to close my eyes as I begin to feel safe. Make sure you can feel the floor or chair under you. It may take time to get all of the mind-trafficking out but don't give up, this can take time.

2. Breath a few times in your nose and out of your mouth. I like to remind myself that God breathed The breath of life into me, and so I will recite these words, "God breathed the breath of life into humans and we became living souls. In-and-out, I am a living soul."

3. Bring your focus to your words or the music playing in the background. I like to listen to music by Alberto & Kimberly Rivera, namely "Capture." If you'd like more music like this to listen to, email me I'd love to help you on this journey. Notice how your body feels and how your legs and feet feel. Notice how your back feels against the chair or surface.

4. Find scriptures like Psalm 23, "The Lord is my shepherd, I have everything I need", for example

5. As the energy shifts, notice how heavy each part of your body feels as you relax those muscles and begin to trust something or someone other than yourself.

6. Feel this sense of heaviness going from your head, down your legs, through your feet, and out into the ground. Focus on the fear or anxiety you may be experiencing and telling yourself "I am trusting the shepherd, who knows everything I need".

You can do this meditation in a private room, in your car on your lunch hour, as I have so often done, on your bed, a chair, couch, anywhere! Something is compelling about connecting with your faith, God, a shepherd who know what you need or even the Earth in this manner.

Meditate

Meditation is a practice of improving your moment-by-moment awareness. Meditation usually begins with appreciating, focusing on, inhaling, and exhaling. However, this doesn't need to be formal or ritualistic. Just simply find a few seconds to focus on your breathing, often before sleep. Also, meditation can be helpful if you ask yourself a set of questions like "What can I do to change?", What am I trying to achieve?", or "How am I going to cope with my fears?"

Get Honest Feedback From Others

Asking someone you fully trust to point out your blind spots can be a really powerful way to up your self-awareness game—but it can also be incredibly painful.

Others often have a better perspective on us than we do, especially friends and family close to us. Asking them simply and safely (by "safe," I mean not exploding and threatening to castrate them for insulting your honor) can lead to great gains in self-awareness.

This is a pro-level move and I don't recommend it for everyone, at least not at first when you're just starting to uncover some inner revealing about yourself.

If you go to your best friend or a trusted family member and ask them to be completely honest about who you are as a person, your personality, and/or some part of your life you're not sure about, what they have to say probably isn't going to be all that easy to hear.

Look, all of us have some unsavory parts of ourselves we'd rather forget about. We all have dysfunctions. We all do stupid, sometimes well. We all have things we'd rather forget. We all hurt, even other people at some point.

So, if you're not ready to have someone judge you for all of that just yet, work on mindfulness and writing first. You need to be able to a) trust someone to tell you the truth and b) not feel attacked when what they tell you is hard to hear. Not everyone can do that easily, but I think it's something to work towards.

Make time for self-reflection

While self-awareness is the ability to see yourself clearly, being able to self-reflect is the willingness to point your attention inward, and explore who it is you are and what you want from life. The difference I point out is that self-awareness is a mindset: it's the approach I have to my inner workings at any given moment. Self-reflection is an activity, one done with intention.

The more attention is directed inward, the more truth is revealed. Over time, you begin to sink below the surface-level thoughts, into deeper parts of being. You'll discover your core values, what is most meaningful to you, what you'd like to achieve, what you need more of, less of, etc.

For the full benefits, clear your schedule and set a deliberate time for self-reflection. You might begin small, with a few hours per week spent alone in nature. Or you might make a self-reflection retreat a regular part of your routine. This is a personal favorite of mine, and something I aim to schedule for several weekends throughout the year.

Suzanne M. Howard

Learn skilled introspection

Not all introspection is equal. Being introspective doesn't necessarily lead to growth. I've always been introspective. For a long time, this introspection was an anxiety-inducing space of rumination and emptiness. Elrich discovered that people"who scored high on self-reflection were more stressed, depressed and anxious, less satisfied with their jobs and relationships, more self-absorbed, and they felt less in control of their lives."

There's a clear difference between self-reflection and insight. The latter is an intuitive understanding of who you are, not aimless rumination. Insight is linked to stronger relationships, a clearer sense of purpose and greater well-being, self-acceptance and happiness.They also felt more in control of their lives and were much more likely to experience rapid personal development.

Identify what triggers your negative emotions

Understanding what makes you mad, sad, stressed, or jealous can go a long way in terms of self-awareness. The reason? When you recognize what sparks your negative emotions, you can become more selective of the people, places, and situations you choose to engage with. It also helps you become more conscious of how you respond to your environment and things you can't control.

To learn more about your triggers, try examining any situation, person, or thing that prompts a negative emotion. For example, you can ask yourself, "What did the other person say that caused me to feel (insert emotion here)? What was my reaction? Is this something I want to feel regularly?" You can then use your responses to make informed decisions that facilitate a more peaceful life,

Question your opinions and beliefs

Challenging your opinions and beliefs is an amazing way to learn about who you are. It increases your awareness of your thoughts, along with the biases and behaviors that stem from those thoughts, says Pruden. It's worth noting this isn't about trying to prove yourself wrong, though. Rather, it's about recognizing the possibility that your opinions and beliefs can change—and giving them a chance to grow.

If you're unsure where to start, ask yourself questions like: "What is the origin of this opinion? Is this opinion beneficial to me or people I love? Is there any truth to my viewpoint?" Asking these questions will allow you to identify and assess your thought patterns.

Identify your emotional kryptonite

Nobody likes to feel sad, anxious, ashamed, or any other kind of difficult emotion. This is understandable since they feel bad—sometimes painfully so!

While we all recoil from painful emotions, each of us tends to have one particular emotion that we especially dislike and try to avoid.. Some will go to extraordinary—sometimes harmful—lengths to distract themselves or numb out that specific feeling of sadness, even if it means intensifying other painful emotions like anxiety, shame, and guilt.

I had a client who discovered that part of the reason he struggled with social anxiety was that he worried constantly that people were judging him. Specifically, he worried that they could tell he drank too much and were judging him for that.

- When I asked him about his drinking, we eventually discovered that even though drinking was causing him a lot of shame and anxiety, to him it was worth it because it was the only way he knew how to distract from the sadness in his life.

- So even though anxiety was the obvious emotion he was struggling with, he eventually became self-aware enough to realize that sadness was the emotion at the root of his struggle. *I am not a clinician or therapist.

We all have certain emotions that we especially dislike—our emotional kryptonite. And more often than not, that means we try very hard to avoid that emotion.

The problem is, being so afraid of an emotion that we're willing to do just about anything to avoid it can lead to some pretty negative consequences in the long term (substance abuse, for instance).

But more importantly, by avoiding the emotion, we're avoiding listening to what the emotion has to say to us. Painful emotions are painful because our mind is trying to get our attention—often for a very good reason.

Learning to tolerate the discomfort of our emotional kryptonite—the feeling you are most afraid to feel—can unlock a wealth of insight about ourselves and our world if w'ere willing to listen.

Learn a new skill

Just like traveling forces us to become more self-aware by throwing us into novel situations, learning something new increases self-awareness by forcing us to think and act in novel ways.

As adults, we all get pretty set in our ways, in large part, because we end up doing the same things over and over again.

And while this leads to a certain kind of comfort, it also fosters a narrowness of mind...

When the only things you're doing are things you're already good at, it's easy to be lulled into a false sense of security that you know how things work.

The antidote is what's sometimes called Beginner's Mind. The idea behind a beginner's mind is that to learn new things, the mind has to be flexible and see things fresh—like a child.

This means that if you want to cultivate flexibility and freshness within yourself and the way you see things (i.e. self-awareness), you should go out of your way to be a beginner. And one of the best ways to do this is to learn a new skill.

Whether it's speaking Italian or learning how to juggle, committing to learning a new skill is a powerful exercise in mental flexibility and self-awareness.

CHAPTER SEVEN
WAYS TO KNOW YOU ARE GROWING IN SELF-AWARENESS

Self-awareness allows you to know your strengths and weaknesses. It helps you understand what triggers negative emotions and what brings you joy. When you have healthy self-awareness, you can reflect on why you feel a certain way and control how your feelings can turn into reactions.

You can empathize with the people around you and find ways to reach your goals amid difficult situations and circumstances. Knowing yourself strengthens your ability to be vulnerable, which allows you to develop stronger relationships with the people entrusted to your care, whether they be family, friends, or colleagues

Fine Tuning

When you fine-tune your self-awareness abilities, you are more adaptable, and you can lead with greater confidence. Psychologist and author Sherrie Campbell, in her book "Loving Yourself: The Mastery of Being Your Person", writes, "Self-awareness keeps us grounded, attuned and focused...When leaders are grounded, they can be efficient and deliberate in staying on task and being attuned to those around them. Leaders who can control their minds and emotions help to guide those around them to develop their self-knowledge and success."

Learning to be aware of yourself isn't always easy but it is one skill that can help you become a much more effective leader. So, how well do you know yourself? How do you know that you are self-aware or at least growing in self-awareness?

You know you are growing in self-awareness when:

1. You can identify your emotions and name what you are feeling.

Emotions, especially when they are negative, tend to take over your mind and body without you realizing it. You lose rational thinking, become defensive, and damage relationships.

When you can identify your emotions, you can begin to question what you need at that moment. Part of identifying your emotions is being able to name what you are feeling. Knowing how to name them and talk about them, with both yourself and with others, is a key to developing self-awareness.

Every day I experience a range of emotions. Sometimes, when I'm feeling frustrated, I get overly critical of myself and my work. Sometimes, when I'm tired, I am less patience with myself and my colleagues and the people entrusted to my care.

In the past, I was less aware of these feelings and would fall into an unhealthy work mode, which was effecting my overall health. Neither my frustration nor my critical reaction helped me feel better or fix the actual problem. But, by improving my self-awareness, I have begun to understand what I'm feeling and how to address the actual things that trigger my emotions.

You can check your emotions at any moment during the day. Ask yourself:

- What emotions am I experiencing at the moment? There are at least 54 different emotions. Learn to identify them with more than the general, sad, glad, or mad categories.

- Am I listening to my body? Is my heart beating faster? Is my stomach churning? Am I losing my voice? What is my body reacting to?

- What causes or triggers some of my negative emotions?

2. You can identify your emotional triggers.

Just as you can know your emotions, you can know what triggers your emotional response. Instead of repressing or denying your emotions, you learn to bend and flex with them, adapting to your situation and processing your emotions before communicating with others.

We each have coping mechanisms that protect us from the hurt, disappointment, and failure that we fear. Unknowingly, we develop these mechanisms from childhood and significant experiences. Being able to recognize when these coping mechanisms begin to take over your thinking and acting is an impactful example of self-awareness.

Have you ever shut down or disengaged in a meeting? Have you ever been in a conversation when you felt irritated, frustrated, or angry? Have you ever caught yourself saying, "I'm not angry? I just feel deeply about this?" Healthy self-awareness knows what triggers your disengagement, frustration, or anger.

What are your most common coping mechanisms? When do you get the most defensive in life? What coping mechanisms did you develop as a child that no longer serve you?

3. You can define and live by your values and beliefs.

Many times, the need to belong and to be liked is stronger than who you are or what you value or believe. You feel so much pressure to fit in with the people around you that you set aside your values and beliefs. You know you are self-aware when you can step back and ask yourself, "Am I being true to myself at this moment?"

It is difficult to ignore all the messages about what you should believe. But the more you develop your self-awareness and determine your core values, the more you can be the leader needed for this time.

What are your core values? When have you tried to please others? When have you based your decision more on the expectations of others rather than your own?

4. You can identify and affirm your strengths.

Sometimes it is intimidating to take a self-assessment or to be evaluated because you are afraid of what you might find out about yourself. Self-awareness is shown in knowing both your strengths and your shortcomings, owning them for yourself, and leaning into your strengths, and getting help with your weaknesses.

Not one of us is perfect. Even the most successful person you know has a list of shortcomings that they had to overcome to achieve their success. Self-awareness is about identifying your strengths and your weaknesses but finding a way to lean into your strengths.

By possessing this self-awareness, you can become a more effective leader, mother, father, spouse, friend, etc. You find strategies and support for your weaknesses, while simultaneously letting your strengths flourish.

What are your strengths? What are your weaknesses? How can you redesign your life or environment to emphasize your strengths?

5. You can celebrate what brings you joy.

With healthy self-awareness, you can identify what brings you joy and make joy a priority in your life. Too often, you know what makes you happy, but you push it off because there are too many important things to do.

The discipline to commit to what brings you joy is not always easy. So, possessing the self-awareness to realize what gives you joy is important. Allow yourself to live into and celebrate what brings you joy.

What gives you joy? How often do you celebrate the joy in your everyday life? What do you put above your joy, and why?

6. You know what you need in your relationships.

It sounds simple, but it is complicated. Relationships are too important not to take into account regarding self-awareness. Too often we limit the potential for healthy and empowering relationships because we have either limited our understanding of relationships or we are afraid of vulnerability. When you don't have a clear understanding of what you need, you end up in frustrating and unfulfilling situations. Healthy self-awareness helps you identify who you need to be for the people around you.

Imagine if you knew exactly what you wanted from a friend, a colleague, a partner, or a family member. If you know what you want or need, then you know how to communicate when you are struggling, lost, or sad in these relationships.

What do you value most in a friendship? How often are you able to express what you need from the people in your life?

Your Turn

So, how well do you know yourself? Becoming self-aware is not as easy as flipping a switch or attending a seminar. It takes time, attention, reflection, and practice. But the more you pause and think about what you feel, want, and need, the more you will experience the life-changing benefits of self-awareness.

Becoming self-aware is critical to your personal and professional growth. Don't let your lack of self-knowledge stagnate your influence. Know yourself.

Take Action

Take 5 minutes at the end of the day to reflect upon the situations and circumstances of the day. Reflect upon one or two of the following (no particular order):

- The meetings you attended

- The people with whom you had interaction

- What emotions did you experience?

- Was anything said or done that triggered a negative response from you?

- When did you have to stand on your values or beliefs? Did you give in?

- When were you aware of your strengths or weaknesses? How did you respond?

- When did you experience joy?

- How did you cultivate relationships today?

- Who do you need to contact to express appreciation for helping you become more who you were created to be?

- Who do you need to contact to ask forgiveness for your lack of self-awareness?

CHAPTER EIGHT
HOW DOES SELF-AWARENESS LEAD TO SUCCESS?

What does success mean to you? This is the dreaded question people hate answering. Finding the right answer to it is a struggle in itself. However, there is a way towards understanding the nuances that come with these questions. Defining success may be a subjective term, it comes with variations and a different set of goals that are unique from one person to another. However, the key ingredient towards getting the right answer lies in self-awareness. This is an aspect that is often missed out on, leaving one in a spiral of confusion and worry.

Many people are struggling with success when it comes to their social lives or economic matters precisely because they're not self-aware enough. This is because self-awareness is doubtlessly one of the key factors of success in today's world, largely because it helps you avoid making errors ahead of time and is a crucial aspect of the introspection that most experts rely upon to keep themselves calm and collected.

Self-awareness is the one known key to being successful in any aspect of life. It could be for relationships, career, business, or overall happiness. Sounds pretty simple, right? It is, only that it is not. Self-awareness is not achieved in a snap. It is a process that a person goes through in life. Also, there's no end to it.

So, if there is no end to it, how does one become successful?

The concepts of self-awareness and success are both subjective and cannot be measured by any other person's yardstick. With this, it is up to you to gauge them and achieve them.

Self-awareness is a person's ability to analyze and recognize one's thoughts and emotions. It is knowing what makes you tick. So what if you know how you feel and what you are thinking? How does self-awareness even relate to success? Unlike what some would think, success does not just fall out of the sky.

To achieve your goals and aspirations sustainably and progressively, it is important to look within. This starts with interpersonal communication. Exploring one's strengths and weakness sets the tone for what one's true potential is. It helps in sharpening and honing the skills and strengths and working on the flaws, both of which when combined, become the building block towards unlocking your true potential. This is how the path to success is then laid out with minimal hurdles and challenges. For instance, if you wish to become a famous violin player one day, reflecting on the internal factors causing a roadblock can help move forward. If it is laziness to practice or clumsiness that makes you misplace your violin bow every time to sit to play, identifying these markers and being aware of them is the first step. From here on, being conscious of your behavior and actions can play an important role in preventing you from slacking. It then opens the way for more practice, adding vigor and luster to your violin playing skills and making the attainment of your goals easier. Thus, helping you become successful.

Yes, we do read a lot of success stories from entrepreneur and business magazines and websites. Who wouldn't want to achieve the same success as those people had? But what we don't see is the hard work they have gone through to achieve their success.

You see, everyone's situation is different. Success is subjective. Without self-awareness, you will continue to envy other people's success and will continue to aspire for the same feat to happen to you.

Self-awareness also provides a solid foundation for success because it encourages careful decision-making and thinking before acting. If you're self-aware, you think things through before you speak or act. You consider what the other person is thinking and feeling. You understand the implications of your words and actions and can choose what is most appropriate.

In addition, self-aware communicators are more emotionally stable. They understand their strong points as well as their limitations. They're not afraid to have weaknesses or vulnerabilities or to ask for help when they need it. Because they can be honest with themselves, they can be honest with others.

Here's why self-awareness is the key to success in your everyday life and some of the ways you can gradually acclimate yourself to become more self-aware.

It starts with mastering your talents

Those of us who are enjoying success in the professional world have long since realized something that many others are struggling with; success starts with mastering your talents. You need to determine what you excel at, find your niche, and work to become one of the leading experts in your field if you ever want to be truly successful as a professional. Similarly, in a non-professional social life, being aware of your talents and skills is an excellent way to start making new friends and becoming more comfortable with yourself.

Thus, it's worth beginning your journey towards self-awareness with meditation and introspection. You can never truly determine what you're great at if you're not brutally honest with yourself; when you're struggling with a certain task, you need to admit it to yourself as plainly as you would accept the fact that you're great at a different task. Even business experts on Wall Street routinely find themselves meditating and relying on introspective methods when they feel stressed or on the edge of a burn-out.

Those who are self-aware are sure of a few things; namely, they're aware of what they're good at, what they love to do, and what they want to be doing in both their near and long-term futures. If you're lacking that kind of certainty, it can be hard to truly achieve success.

After all, whether we're talking about the business world or a personal romantic relationship, someone who doesn't have a vision about where they'll be a few years from now isn't likely to attain success.

The tech-centric nature of the 21st century makes self-awareness an even more important key to success than ever before. That's because our digital gadgets are reshaping us, oftentimes without our knowledge or consent. Some have even labeled the advent of the digital era the "End of Reflection," a period in which were all so caught up with our electronic devices and social media channels that we refuse to ever put our gadgets down and practice the art of introspection.

Success is Relative

Every individual holds a different story. Each person goes through different circumstances and different situations. Success is subjective. When we are not self-aware, we always envy the success of other people and try to pull them down.

Success is a relative concept as it varies from individual to individual. Being self-aware makes you have your idea of success in the first place. For some people, having a lot of money is a success while for others having five or six houses is success. Some people dream of being debt-free while others long for health, happiness, or peace. Similarly, different people achieve their goals or success in different ways. Some become successful in their early years while other people get success in old age. The route to success is different for everyone. We cannot achieve success by creating hatred or by envying others.

Moving towards success

Once you've started down the long and oftentimes challenging road of determining what your skillset is and figuring out what you want to do in the future, you can begin moving towards success. Even after you've begun practicing self-awareness and appreciating introspection in your day-to-day life, you'll need constant checks and reminders to ensure that you're not straying from the path to success.

In these situations, a coach can help keep you on the path and navigate any hurdles that come your way. One of the advantages of modern communications technology is that you can find an online business coach anywhere and use web conferencing technology to receive guidance and advice.

For those who are looking to climb the corporate ladder and make something of themselves professionally, being self-aware is an essential part of remaining on course towards career advancement. Similarly, if you're having trouble navigating a new relationship, being aware of how you come across and the many ways in which others portray you in their heads can help you from making an embarrassing gaffe. Thus, while we're regularly inundated with guides on how to master self-awareness to succeed as a leader, don't let yourself think that introspection and tireless self-reflection should only be relied upon in the workplace and not at home, too.

This is in part because those who are self-aware uniquely understand that there's a fine line between their work and personal lives and that the level of self-awareness you exercise in your professional life is probably indicative of the self-awareness you possess in your personal life, too. Once you begin realizing that how you're perceived at both work and at home blend together to create one constant image for yourself, you'll appreciate the importance of being self-aware even more.

For many folks, constantly trying to be self-aware isn't an easy habit to take up, but it's costless and an excellent way that many people unwind and practice the kind of introspection that's so crucial at attaining true success. It's time to stop committing the same gaffes and fumbling during social interactions time and time again; with the power of self-awareness and introspection on your side, you can become more confident, identify and repair your flaws, and attain success in your personal lives at a new level.

Achieving self-awareness is challenging and a lifelong effort. The earlier you start to work on yourself, the more self-aware you'll become, the more likely "the powers that be" will recognize your leadership potential and accelerate your journey.

To make self-awareness a true advantage in keeping yourself motivated and successful;

i. Invite and accept criticism

There's not a single person who doesn't have some flaw that stands in their way when they strive for success. Big or small, these flaws aren't hurting anybody else except you, so it's in your best interests to dig deep and hear what your shortcomings are. Of course, nobody likes to take criticism, but if you know what your weaknesses are then you'll be better equipped to work on them and improve them. You never know what other areas in your life self-improvement can help! In the end, it's all for your benefit.

ii. Learn from your mistakes

This is another aspect of self-honesty that can be difficult but is essential for entrepreneurial success. There are two parts to learning from your mistakes. First of all, you have to acknowledge what your mistakes were. Take ownership even if in the past you might have tried to shift blame to others. Second of all, you need to implement real changes in how you handle future issues based on the outcomes of previous mistakes. Taking a critical eye to the decisions you've made which perhaps didn't work out well can only help you make better decisions in the future.

So how do you use your self-awareness to achieve success?

First, identify which of your unique characteristics you need to utilize to achieve your definition of success. Take note of the characteristics you need to utilize as strengths or weaknesses. Ideally, you will want to maximize the use of your strengths and supplement these with the continued development of your identified areas for improvement. The more you can utilize your strengths the faster you will achieve your success.

Next, continue developing those areas you identified which are necessary for you to achieve your success. Develop them so you become a master of these strengths. You want people to identify you as a genius in these areas. Develop those areas which you noted are weaknesses but are necessary for you to achieve your success. This is critical for you to achieve your success.

Finally, take action towards your success. You now understand your uniqueness, true definition of success, and what you need to do to achieve your success.

True self-awareness is the complete understanding of yourself, your strengths and weaknesses, and how they relate to your definition of success. You should now understand which of your characteristics are most important in achieving your success. The more self-aware you are the more likely you are to achieve your success.

CHAPTER NINE
SELF-AWARENESS AND
COMMUNICATION

Self-Awareness is having a clear understanding of your personality, your thoughts, emotions, and ultimate behaviors. It allows you to better understand how you affect other people, how they perceive you, and how you ultimately manage your responses to them making sure they are an important part of the conversation.

It rarely occurs to most people that listening is the most important part of communication. If you're all ears and no talk, what kind of communication is going on? A lot! Especially if the listening starts with yourself. And this is what self-awareness is all about. It's not a chapter in new age spiritualism or a state of mind achieved only under hypnosis.

Awareness is the ability to be conscious of the experiences and stimuli that ultimately determine how you take in and process information. What you think, believe, and sense is a reflection of what is already dwelling and stirring within you. Knowing how self-awareness can affect communication can improve every relationship in your life. It's a powerful tool that can facilitate problem-solving and resolution of deep-seated issues.

Self-awareness allows for listening that is free of assumptions and judgments that compromise healthy communication. Before we can listen deeply to others, we need to learn how to listen deeply to ourselves. It is this self-awareness that helps us to understand the other's frame of reference. Increasing your self-awareness allows you to communicate more honestly, with greater openness to the feedback you might receive. As a consequence, you will communicate more effectively with those around you.

Here are some examples of the connection between self-awareness and communication:

- Self-awareness means that you know how your thoughts, emotions, and behaviors affect others and you're able to manage yourself so that the other person is an important part of the conversation.

- Self-awareness helps you be more comfortable with yourself so you can relate to others with genuine confidence and kindness.

- Self-awareness allows you to get out of the way and let people tell you what's important to them without letting your stuff complicate the interaction.

- Self-awareness gives you the ability to shift from always having to talk (the result of ego) to listening to people instead.

- Self-awareness helps you communicate with others on a deeper level because you make them feel valued and important.

- Self-awareness helps you understand how others see you and how you can adapt to make more meaningful connections and build stronger relationships.

- Self-awareness helps you collaborate with others.

HOW DOES SELF-AWARENESS AFFECT OUR INTERNAL FILTERS?

When you think of being "self-aware" you may have flashbacks to self-help books and guided meditations. But would you even consider how self-awareness can affect communication with the people in your life? Would it dawn on you that your ability — and willingness — to know yourself can improve your ability to know others?

If you're stuck in the perception that communication is all about what you say, you'll miss out on how self-awareness can affect communication.

It rarely occurs to most people that listening is the most important part of communication. If you're all ears and no talk, what kind of communication is going on? _____

Self-awareness, in a nutshell, is looking at your internal filters and making sense of them. Your life experiences, beliefs, values, assumptions, biases, fears, and expectations all influence how you listen. And how you listen is the key to how self-awareness can affect communication.

There are three parts to this internal experience: your thoughts, your emotions, and your bodily sensations.

Thinking, as you would imagine, is connected to the mind, while sensing is connected to the body. Intersecting the two is feeling — the emotional component that can be affected by your thoughts, but isn't always logical.

Self-awareness is your ability to recognize and separate these different experiences so you can address each for what it is.

Think about the last heated argument you had with someone — the kind of argument that left you feeling out of control, flushed, confused, exhausted. Can you remember what you thought, felt, sensed? Or did it all run together and intensify an already intense situation?

Did you find yourself saying things without thinking first? Tossing around accusations and assumptions as if they were facts? Perhaps not being able to distinguish what was coming from within yourself from what was coming from the other person?

Most importantly, did you find it difficult to listen — deeply listen — to the other person? If you were asked to repeat what the other person said and to express understanding of it, would your mirroring be accurate? Or would it reflect your personal experiences, biases, feelings, disappointments?

Self-awareness is the antidote to this internal flooding. Especially in situations of conflict, it isolates and identifies your internal filters. It helps you to know what is happening inside of you. Am I projecting my thoughts onto this person? Am I feeling a specific emotion like anger or sadness? Is my body giving me signals like numbness or flushing?

Knowing how self-awareness can affect communication can improve every relationship in your life. It's a powerful tool that can facilitate problem-solving and resolution of deep-seated issues.

Go back to that heated argument and try to remember things that were said and reactions to them.

Phrases like "I feel like you" and "you never/always/don't" are land mines when it comes to effective communication. They muddle the internal experiences of thoughts, feelings, and sensations, leaving the speaker confused, the listener defensive, and the situation more intense.

Imagine now how that argument would have sounded if you were able to separate the components of your interior experience.

What if you had been able to recognize your sadness as a feeling and your assumption of lack of love as a thought? And what if, instead of saying, "I feel like you don't care about or love me," you spoke with clarity out of your self-awareness? "I feel very sad, and what I am making up in my mind is that you don't love me anymore. Is that true?"

By recognizing the components of your own inner life, you're far more likely to take ownership of it.

"I feel like you" is a side-door introduction of thought — an assumption, an accusation. But feelings are feelings — they aren't always logical and they don't need to be justified or defended. They simply 'are. '

Thoughts, however, are the seat of our judgments, assumptions, and biases. They are closely connected to our beliefs, which form a frame of reference for how we see the world.

If you want to understand how self-awareness can affect communication, you need to understand the distinctions and interrelations between these interior players.

And, just as importantly, you need to accept responsibility for that inner experience that only you have. It's up to you to identify it for what it is and then express it clearly, authentically, honestly, and compassionately.

The deep yearning within any relationship is to feel heard — deeply, soulfully heard — and understood. At its purest level, all communication is an outreach for this satisfaction.

But we are not mind-readers, no matter how close we may be in our relationships. So it's incumbent upon each of us to listen — deeply listen — to what accumulates and stirs within ourselves.

Then and only then can we hope to communicate accurately what we long to have safely, and lovingly reflected from us.

And in that reflection lies the hope of resolution, healing, and moving forward.

SELF-AWARENESS HELPS TO HANDLE OUR THOUGHTS AND FEELINGS?

Self-awareness is a key communication skill that teaches you how to handle your feelings and to manage them. Without this skill, it can be difficult or impossible for you to know what other people are feeling and what those feelings might mean.

Self-awareness is a form of self-reflection that allows us to know our internal feelings, motivations, and desires. It helps us recognize the relationship between our attitudes (thoughts), feelings (emotions), intentions, and behaviors. By having self-awareness we can keep a watchful eye on ourselves and our behavior to avoid making harmful decisions or harmful mistakes.

So here are reasons why self-awareness is important in communication.

1. It helps us to understand ourselves better.

You need to understand yourself better because it allows you to know what your needs are and how your thoughts and feelings affect your actions today and tomorrow. Without self-awareness, we cannot know what is going on with our emotions or our thoughts, which makes it hard for us to make healthy choices or make positive changes in our lives.

If you don't know yourself, then you have no idea why or what your actions are leading to. If you don't know yourself, how can you fix the problems that have led to these mistakes? How can you avoid making similar mistakes in the future?

2. It helps us to understand others better.

Self-awareness also helps us to understand other people better because it allows us to know and understand our thoughts and feelings towards that person. This allows us to better understand their feelings and the level of concern they are experiencing. In turn, this will help us to know what our behavior should be and how to respond appropriately.

3. It helps us to control our emotions.

Self-awareness also allows us to control our emotions and productively use them to strengthen personal relationships or manage conflict. Self-awareness helps us to control emotions and not let them gain the upper hand. If you are emotional you will be more likely to make decisions that are not in line with your values.

4. It helps us to communicate effectively.

We have all made mistakes in communication at least once or twice, often during stressful times when we are feeling hurt, angry, or insecure because of something that has happened or is happening in our life. Self-awareness helps us to communicate clearly and effectively so that we can express ourselves appropriately. This also allows us to avoid hurting each other unnecessarily.

5. It allows us to understand our motives.

Self-awareness allows us to know our motives and how they can affect the way we see others. It is important for you not only to understand your motives but also what you are trying to do with them as well as the effects of it and how it worked out in the end.

6. It allows us to set individual goals.

Being self-aware allows us to set individual goals based on our own needs and desires rather than the expectations of others, because we are aware of ourselves, we know what is important to the self so we can make changes accordingly for our benefit.

"Self-awareness gives you a feeling of control over your life, and that brings dignity. If you are self-aware, you are aware of days that you may feel like giving up. When you're self-aware, you realize that your life is not over; that there's going to be another day. It becomes a source of strength."

7. Self-Awareness allows us to avoid obsessive-compulsive disorder (OCD).

The greatest form of self-awareness is being able to maintain your own identity without letting others define you. You can be aware of how you react and behave, so you do not become your actions. Being self-aware allows us to avoid obsessive-compulsive issues by not allowing ourselves, our minds and bodies to fall into the patterns of having to meet certain expectations to feel cherished or loved.

8. It allows us to avoid Escaping Reality.

We are not what we do, we are who we are and what we think. We cannot control how our minds work nor can we control our bodies, but that does not mean you should accept them unconditionally. Our thoughts and actions cause others to react in certain ways to which your response will change the outcome of the situation or cause you more harm than good.

9. You are not your mind/brain

The brain is constrained in several ways, but it can easily be freed from those constraints just as it can and should be freed from the constraints imposed upon you by others. The brain can be freed from negative feelings or harmful thoughts because it is not limited to them and does not have to be.

"You can change your mind, so you control your brain." — Bill Wilson

10. It allows us to overcome the struggle of being "self-conscious".

Every time you need to become more self-aware, then you have overcome the struggle of being self-conscious and this is just one more reason why self-awareness is so important.

How to Improve your Social Communication Skills:

One effective way to improve your social communication skills is by modeling. You should try to observe a confident person who communicates well and try to model their actions and strategies. Try to do what a successful communicator does.

One reason why this is so helpful is that just about everyone experiences fear or nervousness in communicative situations. This is especially true when communicating in a group, for example, in meetings, presentations, or speeches. It is therefore helpful to understand how "confident" communicators deal with these fears and appear confident.

First, think about the social situations which you find difficult. Decide how you would like to relate with others socially and watch someone you admire who is socially skillful. If you watch carefully you may notice how they smile and listen to others a lot. How does he or she relax and speak clearly? What is it about them that shows confidence? How does this person act to feel confident when communicating?

You can learn to be a good speaker and a good communicator and your social and professional relationships will improve tremendously. This will not only boost your self-awareness but will also have many positive effects on other areas of your professional and personal life.

CHAPTER TEN
WHY DO MOST PEOPLE LACK SELF-AWARENESS?

What does lack of awareness mean?. Lack of awareness is a major problem that deteriorates our quality of life, as it affects the vision we have of ourselves and prevents us from functioning properly in society. Lack of self-awareness is an annoying emotion that blocks us in decisions and actions.

If you suffer from a lack of self-awareness, it is important to discover what causes this in you. If you can identify why you lack awareness, you can begin to take steps to improve this area. Some of the causes of lack of self-awareness are fear of criticism, self-doubt, lack of assertiveness, and perfectionism. When you lack self-awareness, it's because you are having unrealistic expectations from others standards of opinion.

1. Fear of criticism

The cause of fear of criticism is that you are too concerned about others opinions and that makes you feel insecure. Instead of taking critique as feedback, you tend to take it otherwise and you become defensive. When you care too much what others think you are open to manipulation. When you care less what others think you become a more honest person because you don't have to pretend. When you have gotten over that inferiority complex you'll just feel better about yourself regardless of 'the facts.

This will stop you from assuming you're not as good as others and help you accept your areas of strength as well as weakness with objectivity and calm.

2. Lack of assertiveness

If you can't express your needs and stand up for yourself you become resentful and angry. Lack of assertiveness creates insecurity, doubt, and pessimism. When you learn to become assertive people will realize that you know your mind and they will give you more respect and consider you capable of more responsibility. You will be treated with more respect and you will feel better about yourself.

3. Perfectionism

Perfectionism leads to having unrealistic expectations of yourself from the standards and opinions of others. Thinking that you can't do something unless is perfect is an unrealistic way to approach everyday life. It is also a way of avoiding making mistakes that create more insecurity.

Experiencing too much pressure from your parents or even a friend to meet the demands and expectations that they set out for you causes a lack of self-awareness. Setting unrealistic goals and fear of failure is another factor.

SIGNS YOU LACK SELF-AWARENES

A lack of self-awareness is perhaps our most significant enemy to self-growth.

I'm sure you can name someone in your life who lacks self-awareness. The most egregious examples of lacking self-awareness are easy to spot. The people make excuses, have emotional outbursts, and give answers unrelated to the actual question. But the truth is, the majority of us lack self-awareness in everyday life. Research has shown that 95% of people think they're self-aware. In reality, only 10-15% of us are.

Fortunately for you, you can change this. Once you accept that you probably lack self-awareness, you can start to look for the signs in your life. Then, you can learn how to change them to achieve the growth that you want.

Why change a lack of self-awareness?

Have you heard of the phrase "Ignorance is bliss?" It can be tempting to avoid topics like self-awareness. After all, it can be incredibly scary to look within ourselves and search for the truth. I mean, what if we don't like what we find?

Lacking self-awareness might make us feel safe, but it's hurting us far more than it's helping.

Possessing self-awareness can have life-changing effects on our life. These changes aren't just in the moment either; they are long-lasting. Lacking self-awareness holds us back in our work, our happiness, our relationships, and our emotional well-being.

Throughout my life, I've always been super introspective. I love to look inward and figure out why I am the way I am. However, introspection does not equal self-awareness. It wasn't until the last couple of years that I became much more self-aware.

When you lack self-awareness, you fail to identify what you're feeling and how it manifests itself in your daily actions. You fail to see the patterns in your behaviors and thinking. As a result, you tend to experience more negative emotions because you don't know how to better align your choices with what you want.

We live in an age of echo chambers online—and that makes it hard to determine if you lack self-awareness. We are so easily inclined to believe our opinions are always right because the net makes it easy for us to find dozens of others who have the same beliefs we do.

That being said, you should always step outside your echo chamber online and listen to what others have to say. When you refuse to listen to others, especially when they are trying to be genuine or offer up proof to their statements, you're doing yourself a disservice.

A key to being self-aware is the ability to look outside your perspective, impartially look at facts, and be open to new ideas. If you fly into a rage when you hear people who have different ideas from you, you lack self-awareness.

When people challenge your ideas or offer feedback, you get defensive or come up with excuses.

This goes hand-in-hand with being an active listener. When you lack self-awareness, it's very common to take things that are meant to be helpful as an attack on your character or intelligence.

Genuine, objective feedback can help you become a better person, and improve your skillset. Refusing to accept it gracefully or take it into account means you lack awareness about your skills. If you're caught making a mistake and lack self-awareness, you'll make excuses as to why it happened. Excuses don't allow for personal growth and often make the entire situation worse. By taking the blame, you are giving yourself an opportunity for growth. You need to know both your strengths and weaknesses to succeed, after all.

1. People often call you a bully.

You might not see yourself as one, but make no mistake about it. Bullying is in the eye of the beholder. A person who acts like a bully, be it through actively hurting others or by pushing others around subconsciously, is not a good thing.

Bullying behavior means that you either don't care about how others see you, that you are actively avoiding issues that are deeply hurting you by hurting others, or that you lack the ability to put yourself in others' shoes. Either way, it's a sign you lack self-awareness on a grand scale.

2. You are very passive-aggressive.

Believe it or not, passive-aggressive behavior is not usually a sign of a healthy mindset. It's a behavior style that deflects from issues that are bothering you, but you might not have the guts to confront. You might not even know what the problem is; you just want to avoid anything near it altogether.

Do you know why you're passive-aggressive? A little introspection may help you overcome this behavior, and make you more capable of communicating your needs with others—just be sure to ask yourself if you are emotionally equipped with great defenses or making excuses and acting out.

3. You don't "get" most people.

Do the actions of people just not make sense to you? Have people told you that you don't understand how social matters work? If peoples' reactions to you don't make sense, or if you can't understand where they're coming from, chances are you lack self-awareness.

Most people have reactions that can be easily understood if you take a look at how you'd react in their position. You also can figure out how your actions are perceived if you practice more introspection— that can help you learn how to relate to others better.

4. You don't understand why you act the way you do.

A good indicator that you lack self-awareness deals with how well you understand your emotions, actions, and behavior. People who lack self-awareness often feel constantly off-kilter, anxious, or angry. They usually can't even pinpoint what upsets them half the time.

Do you find yourself unable to explicitly explain why you are upset? You might also not be able to understand why you behave the way you do if you look at past experiences in your life. Awareness is not an image, and being self-aware is so much easier when you understand that.

5. You have an urge to control everything.

Self-aware people know that no man is an island, and also that they're not always right. They are normally more okay with giving up control, trusting others, and being able to mitigate the anxiety that comes with not knowing all the answers.

If you don't have a decent level of self-awareness, the risk becomes a threat. A person who can't help but micromanage others and control every little detail doesn't realize how badly this affects everyone around them—and how counter-productive it can be.

6. You are prone to emotional outbursts.

Emotional outbursts happen for a wide range of reasons, most of which involve a lack of self-control and self-awareness. For the most part, emotionally intelligent people can control themselves and understand their emotions.

When you don't have much self-awareness, you can't figure out why you feel the way you do. You also might not realize what the consequences of an outburst can be—or even care.

7. It's hard for you to keep friends long-term.

Friends are the people you have around you that "get" you, support you, and make you feel good. Most people are always down for new friends, but when you're not self-aware, they don't stick around.

A surefire sign of something wrong is a revolving door of friendships. If people can't ever seem to stick around, there's a pretty good chance that the recursive loop of self-awareness is causing you to do something to drive them away.

8. You get defensive when receiving feedback.

It's our natural tendency to reject feedback when we receive it. We want to protect our pride. Not to mention, we listen to confirmation bias and struggle to accept information that contradicts us.

Beneath it all, however, is a fear of vulnerability that's causing a lack of self-awareness.

Receiving feedback is tough. We can't help but focus on the negative pieces of information. This taps into some of our primal fears of not belonging and not being good enough. We switch into defensive mode when people tell us something about ourselves that we don't already know. This defensiveness might manifest in the form of making excuses, lashing out, being passive-aggressive, or trying to control others.

Because we're built to lack self-awareness, we need feedback to understand ourselves better. If you find yourself fighting against feedback, ask yourself why this is. If you are self-aware, more feedback will simply help you better understand what you already know

9. You haven't found a way to be consistently successful.

You might think it's bold to declare you should be able to be consistently successful. After all, life is unpredictable and throws a lot of obstacles at us. But how you handle these obstacles and maneuver toward success can be consistent.

If you're consistently facing the same challenges over and over again, failing to achieve success, you probably lack self-awareness.

Being self-aware won't magically make challenges go away. It will, however, help you understand yourself well enough to know what you can do. You can identify your strengths and weaknesses. Then, you can create environments and situations that will highlight your strengths and diminish the impact of your weaknesses. Even how you dress can affect your awareness.

Over the years, I've found out that I'm extremely disciplined and organized. These skills have helped me tackle projects in my personal life and in my professional life that bring my skills to the forefront. As I've grown, I've learned that "big picture" ideas sometimes challenge me because I care more about completion. Knowing this, I can tap into my self-awareness to know when I'll be in my comfort zone, and when I need to find myself some extra support.

10. Nothing is ever your fault.

Be honest with yourself. Do you know you've messed up in the past, but haven't been able to take the blame? People who are not self-aware often don't see themselves at fault, or may even live in denial of the problems they cause.

Chances are, if you really, truly think you lack self-awareness, you're probably right. So, maybe it's time for a little introspection?

11. Your emotional reaction doesn't match the situation

Have you ever felt a strong emotional reaction that felt larger than the situation required? Perhaps you went into a nervous breakdown about a new bit of news, or maybe you flew into a rage at something your friend did (or didn't) do.

If your emotional reaction doesn't match the situation, you're more than likely lacking self-awareness. Your extreme emotions were triggered by something much more deeply rooted than the present events.

12. You repeat negative emotional patterns

Emotions are incredibly complicated to recognize and control. That's because they're rooted in some of the deepest parts of our brain wiring. Because they're so deeply rooted, it's easy to lose sight of what's causing them. And if we don't know what's causing them, we can't do anything to stop them.

A clear sign of lacking self-awareness is if you find yourself repeating negative emotional patterns.

These negative emotional patterns are different for everyone. Some of you might fall into fits of anxiety and panic; others might become super lonely or depressed. Do you tend to get super worked up and critical over my relationship conflicts (even if they were tiny)? The reason these patterns repeat themselves is that you aren't able to recognize what's going on.

The more self-aware you are, the more likely you'll be able to do two things. First, you'll identify that you're in a negative emotional pattern. Second, you'll be able to recognize what caused this pattern and what might need to change to prevent it.

13. The things you do to "make yourself feel better" don't make you feel better.

We all fill our time with hobbies, time-wasters, and behaviors that are supposed to make us feel better. For you, this might be having a glass of wine at the end of a long day. For others, it's taking a mental break and scrolling through social media.

If you are self-aware, you can be intentional with these actions as a means of self-care. However, a clear sign that you lack self-awareness is when "these feel better" behaviors don't make you feel better.

Lack of self-awareness becomes particularly evident when we're feeling extra stressed or low. We want to mask our negative emotions with distractions. When I used to feel uncertain about something in my life, I tried to regain a sense of control by diving into work. The focused hours, however, didn't make me feel any better or help me solve my problems.

Whatever you try to numb your emotions with (whether it's work, alcohol, TV, etc.), it merely takes you away from the main problem you have to deal with. Ultimately, it adds to your lack of self-awareness.

DANGERS CAUSED BY LACK OF SELF-AWARENESS

Have you ever run across someone who you felt was lacking in self-awareness?

This type of individual can be anywhere – home, work, church, etc., simply wherever your circle of acquaintances is you just might have seen this individual.

You may have witnessed mistakes they've made or wondered how they are where they are in your organization, especially if they're in a leadership role.

Someone said this about Daniel Goleman:

"He's the "guru" of emotional intelligence, identified self-awareness as being made up of emotional awareness, accurate self-assessment, and self-confidence. In other words, it is all about knowing your emotions, your strengths and weaknesses, and having a strong sense of your worth."

If we don't have self-awareness, then it can be difficult for us to build upon a solid foundation of our character and apply the right teachings, development, knowledge, direction, and ultimately contribution.

We can all testify that from an emotional standpoint, we've not batted a thousand when we needed to act a certain way in conversations, heated moments of verbal exchanges, or our behavior when emotions run high.

When emotions run high, often, judgment runs low.

These mistakes, if not corrected, form a perception of who we are to ourselves and others as a lack of maturity, self-discipline, self-control, and of course self-awareness.

Think about it.

Do you know anyone who you consider a 'hot-head'? We avoid conflict with these types of people because we have seen how they act in the middle of it.

We shake our heads when we see them interacting with others in this way because we realize they haven't learned and corrected their behavior.

If we aren't careful, just like anything, this can happen to us.

So here are the dangers to avoid that cause a lack of self-awareness:

1. Pride

This one is probably a 'no-brainer', however, it's extremely necessary to avoid. It was the first sin and it's the root of all sin.

Pride in someone who lacks self-awareness is detrimental because of other factors that play into it. If you lack self-awareness, you may not know you're puffed up with pride. You'll conduct yourself in a way that you think is normal and right, yet causes a stench to those around you.

2. Being unteachable

This probably can be interchanged with pride in the battle of which should come first. If you aren't able to listen to the instruction of mentors, teachers, parents, pastors, close friends, etc., then you cannot learn and grow in such a way that is beneficial to your character.

Being unteachable is something we must learn early in life because if we don't, we'll move through it under the assumption that no one can tell us anything as we already know it all. (We all remember those teenage years, right?)

Recognizing that others have valuable insight and assistance to pour into you and being able to receive that is not present in those who are unteachable.

3. Closed Off

Being closed off to others can stem from a myriad of things. Normally, it comes from a place where trust has been broken. Often, those who didn't violate trust pay the price of a closed-off spirit.

Not allowing yourself to form bonds, trust people, and develop that part of your life that is vital to our existence will create false realities in your world. This leads to isolation and exclusion. When you're isolated, you have no example to measure yourself against. You develop hardness and a callous spirit where nothing can penetrate to bring hope and light.

4. Lack of Discipline

We've probably all been there at some point where we echo Paul's words to the Romans when he told them, there's good that I know I should be doing, but I don't do. The things I shouldn't be doing, that's what I find myself doing.

- It's the easy path.

- It's the way that doesn't cost as much.

- It's the things that don't take a lot of time or energy or pain.

The lack of discipline shows up in our lives when we want and know we should be spending time doing things that grow us, and stretch us, yet we rationalize not doing so because of a temporary issue.

- We rationalize not working out because we've spent all day working and we're tired.

- We rationalize not investing in ourselves because we have other obligations.

- We rationalize and justify days that turn into months and years.

This is created because we not only look around and compare ourselves to people who are higher on this climb than us, but we think we have to go from A to Z in a day or a week.

When we aren't able to measure up in these areas in our minds, we quit before we start.

CHAPTER ELEVEN
EMOTIONAL INTELLIGENCE

WHAT IS EMOTIONAL INTELLIGENCE?

Have you ever known people who always seem to keep their cool, who can handle even the most awkward social situations with grace, and who always seem to make others feel at ease? Chances are pretty high that those individuals possess what psychologists refer to as emotional intelligence.

Emotional intelligence involves the ability to understand and manage emotions. Experts agree that this type of intelligence plays an important role in success, and some have suggested that emotional intelligence, or EQ, might even be more important than IQ. In any case, research has suggested that possessing emotional intelligence skills is linked to everything from decision-making to academic achievement.

* EI is a subset of Social Intelligence with the ability to accurately screen self- emotions and emotions of another person while having the reflective ability to discriminate between both to control self-emotions to promote emotional and intellectual growth.

If this description is applied to women, it would mean that women should develop the ability to screen their own emotions and be able to control them. What are emotions? Emotions are subjective mental and physiological states in an individual that varies continuously from positive, negative, and sometimes even contradictorily.

Has your EI reached the level where and when at any point in your life you can analyze yourself as to why you are happy, unhappy, or happy - unhappy at the same time? Let's assume that you incline contradictory emotions most of the time. Are you able after self-analysis to bring those contradictory emotions under control? The answers to these questions are indicators of the level and psychological health and maturity of your EI. If at this stage your answers are unsure then no matter how intelligent (academically or professionally) you consider yourself to be, your EI is at the first stage and needs urgent attention. It is at this level that many women (it also applies to men) become emotional casualties even though they may be at the peak of their careers.

In short, they fail to understand their own emotions and therefore are unable to control them leading to erroneous thinking, decisions, and behaviors that ultimately affect them and those around them.

Some women (including men) are great in self-analysis and self-control. What about their reflective ability to discriminate between their emotions and the emotions of others? This stage of EI is well highlighted by the concepts of transactional analysis in the form of a parent, adult, and child (PAC) emotional states and interactions. PAC refers to the different emotional and interaction states that every one of us is at any point in time. The parent's emotional state is instructive, protective, and highly automatic in its responses. The adult emotional state is responsible, objective, and meditative. The child's emotional state is spontaneous, creative, and can be rebellious. Let's apply these emotional states and interactions to a fictitious scenario.

Let's assume you are a motherly-kind of a wife who is always lecturing your husband about getting drunk. Your EI is in the parent emotional and interaction state. The EI of your drunkard husband is in the child emotional and interaction state. As long as your husband accepts your lectures as a child would do there will be no conflicts.

But let's say one day he is sober and was reflecting on his drunkard behaviors as an adult (adult emotional and interaction state). But you were insensitive to your husband's adult emotional and interaction state and started rattling off your usual lectures. But this time out of irritation at your nagging, he turns around and lashes (child emotional and interaction state) back at you. And you in your righteous indignation (parent emotional and interaction state) lash back at him. What would be the consequences? You can guess it for yourself.

The conflicts between you and your husband are not solely because you are right and he is wrong. It is because of your insensitive emotional state and interaction. You allowed the wrong emotions to be expressed due to insensitivity and conditioning.

Let's assume, if you had displayed an adult emotional and interaction state, your husband would have responded as an adult and instead of conflict, you would have had a wonderful communication on the same wavelength. This is what is meant by EI that is reflective in its ability to discriminate between one's own emotions and the emotions of others. And this is stage two in EI. Are you at this stage? If you have developed your EI at the first stage then it would be very productive if you go on to stage two.

Emotional intelligence affects:

i. Your physical health

If you're unable to manage your emotions, you are probably not managing your stress either. This can lead to serious health problems. Uncontrolled stress raises blood pressure, suppresses the immune system, increases the risk of heart attacks and strokes, contributes to infertility, and speeds up the aging process. The first step to improving emotional intelligence is to learn how to manage stress.

ii. Your mental health

Uncontrolled emotions and stress can also impact your mental health, making you vulnerable to anxiety and depression. If you are unable to understand, get comfortable with, or manage your emotions, you'll also struggle to form strong relationships. This in turn can leave you feeling lonely and isolated and further exacerbate any mental health problems.

iii. Your relationships

By understanding your emotions and how to control them, you're better able to express how you feel and understand how others are feeling. This allows you to communicate more effectively and forge stronger relationships, both at work and in your personal life.

iv. Your social intelligence

Being in tune with your emotions serves a social purpose, connecting you to other people and the world around you. Social intelligence enables you to recognize friend from foe, measure another person's interest in you, reduce stress, balance your nervous system through social communication, and feel loved and happy.

HISTORY OF EMOTIONAL INTELLIGENCE

In the 1940s, David Wechsler, an American Psychologist identified that to be successful, one must be proficient in non-cognitive intelligence. He believed that an individual must understand the outcomes of his own emotions and the emotions of others to be successful. The field of cognition and effect emerged, which popularized the examination of how emotions interacted with thoughts

Until the 1960s, Emotional Intelligence was a social construct that an individual's intelligence is determined through their IQ. However, studies conducted by psychology have constantly refuted the presumption of intelligence being based solely on IQ. Since the inception of the topic of emotional intelligence, countless studies have been conducted to corroborate or impugn the significance of feelings to the individual.

The concept of emotional intelligence was first described in a doctoral dissertation by Wayne Payne entitled "A Study of Emotion: Developing emotional intelligence; self-integration; relating to fear, pain, and desire". This was one of the first notable dissertations which discussed the principles of emotional intelligence. However, Payne's research instigated controversy as to whether emotion or physiological reaction is of more importance.

It was not until the 1990s where the concept of social intelligence would receive a greater appeal. Emotional Intelligence was identified as a form of social intelligence in 1990 by Peter Salovey and John D. Mayer. Peter Salovey and John D. Mayer published an article titled "Emotional Intelligence" in the journal Imagination, Cognition, and Personality". It was described as a "form" of social-intelligence that involves the ability to monitor one's own and other's feelings and emotions, to discriminate among them, and to use this information to guide one's thinking and action". A book entitled "Emotional Intelligence", that was written by Daniel Goleman popularize the notion of emotional intelligence. Goldman defined emotional intelligence as theability to identify, assess, and control one's own emotions, the emotion of others and that of groups".

Goleman believed that only 20% of our success is attributable to our IQ and that 80% of our success is attributed to our EQ (Emotional Quotient). The emotional quotient determines the qualities of an individual which are related to self-motivation, persistence, impulse control, and the regulation of emotions. Goleman's novel analyzed the interrelation between the cognitive and emotional mechanisms in the brain with employee performance. This developed into "Goleman's Theory of IQ", which substantiates the five essential pillars of emotional intelligence.

THE PILLARS OF EMOTIONAL INTELLIGENCE

Emotional intelligence includes 5 different pillars that determine our ability to navigate our emotional world. These pillars include self-awareness, self-regulation, empathy (other awareness"), social skills, and motivation.

When we think of "intelligence," we often associate it with things like logic, math, and science.

However, according to psychologist Daniel Goleman in his influential book Emotional Intelligence: Why It Can Matter More Than IQ, "emotional intelligence" (EQ) is another aspect of intelligence that is often overlooked.

The basic view of emotional intelligence is that emotions aren't necessarily the opposite of thinking, but a different way of thinking about different types of problems that exist in our world. At certain times, emotions can be a valuable tool to help guide our choices and behaviors. But we have to learn how to use them wisely.

In light of his theory of evolution, Charles Darwin theorized that our minds have evolved to experience emotions so that we can better adapt to our environment. For example, we've evolved to experience a "negative" emotion such as fear so that we can better respond to a situation that is bad for survival. In this case, fear is an emotion that motivates us to avoid something when we are in danger.

On the other hand, a "positive" emotion, such as joy, can signal to us that a situation is good for survival. In this case, joy is an emotion that motivates you to seek more of something.

This is a very basic and rudimentary analysis – and it doesn't come anywhere near describing the complexities of our emotional world (as well as the social world) – but it gives you an idea of how different emotions can guide our behaviors in different ways.

Emotional intelligence is about being more aware of our emotions and what they are signaling to us. Below you'll find descriptions of the 5 fundamental pillars that make up emotional intelligence

1. Self-Awareness

The first pillar of emotional intelligence is paying attention to your own emotions.

Emotions often come in two main parts:

1) The psychological component – the thoughts, attitudes, and beliefs that underlie most of our emotions, and

2) The physical component – the bodily sensations that often accompany different emotional states.

For example, an emotion such as nervousness may be a mixture of certain thoughts ("I'm not good at this" or "I'm scared I'm going to make a mistake") and certain sensations in our bodies (a fluttery feeling in our stomach, ie "I have butterflies in my stomach").

Sometimes just being more aware of our emotional states (and all their components) is enough to manage them better. In one recent study, they found simply labeling negative emotions can help you overcome them.

The next time you're feeling a really strong emotion, try stepping back and just observing that emotion as it is. Ask yourself, "What am I feeling? What am I thinking? What physical sensations am I experiencing with this emotion?"

A little honest reflection of your emotions can help you understand yourself better and how your mind works.

2. Self-Regulation

Once you are more aware of your emotions, the next pillar of emotional intelligence is learning how to respond to them better.

In addition to being aware of your own emotions and the impact you have on others, emotional intelligence requires you to be able to regulate and manage your emotions.

This doesn't mean putting emotions on lockdown and hiding your true feelings—it simply means waiting for the right time and place to express them. Self-regulation is all about expressing your emotions appropriately.

Those who are skilled in self-regulation tend to be flexible and adapt well to change. They are also good at managing conflict and diffusing tense or difficult situations.

Depending on the situation, there are many different strategies we can use to better regulate our emotions. Some of these strategies include:

- Channeling an emotion in a new and constructive way, such as through exercising, writing, or painting.

- Avoiding triggers – such as certain people, situations, or environments – that are more likely to bring out negative emotion.

- Seeking positive experiences to reverse negative ruts (such as watching a comedy movie when we are feeling down, or listening to motivating music when we are lazy).

- Turning emotions around by doing the opposite of what you feel.

- Sitting and watching emotions as a passive observer, instead of acting on them impulsively.

These are all strategies available to us to help us regulate our emotions better on an everyday basis.

Think of "emotional intelligence" as a kind of toolkit. There are many different ways to respond to a particular emotion, and not every tool is going to work depending on what the situation is.

The more emotionally intelligent you become, the better you will be at deciding what is the best way to respond to an emotion. But that's going to take steady practice and awareness.

3. Empathy

Understanding your own emotions is half of emotional intelligence, the other half is understanding the emotions of others. As we improve "self-awareness," we also improve "other awareness." We learn that there is sometimes a difference between our thoughts and feelings and the thoughts and feelings of others.

Empathy is our ability to see things from another persons perspective – and to take into account their thoughts and feelings about an experience.It also involves your responses to people based on this information. When you sense that someone is feeling sad or hopeless, how do you respond? You might treat them with extra care and concern, or you might make an effort to buoy their spirits.

Of course, we can never understand another person's mind completely, but we can actively learn about a person's inner thoughts and feelings by paying attention to what they are communicating verbally and non-verbally.

Empathy is a kind of "mind-reading," but it's based on making inferences about people's internal worlds based on their external actions.

Being empathetic also allows you to understand the power dynamics that often influence social relationships, especially in workplace settings. This is important for guiding your interactions with different people you encounter each day.

Those competent in this area can sense who possesses power in different relationships. They also understand how these forces influence feelings and behaviors. Because of this, they can accurately interpret different situations that hinge on such power dynamics.

Another powerful tool for improving empathy is perspective-taking. This is a mental exercise where you imagine yourself experiencing a situation from another person's perspective to better understand them.

Be more willing to ask yourself, "What is this person thinking? What is this person feeling? Why is this person acting in the way they do?" These types of questions will be a great starting point in building more empathy in your daily relationships.

4. Social Skills

Once you understand the emotions of yourself and others, the next question is "How do I respond to other people's emotions?" This is where social skills come in as the last pillar of emotional intelligence.

Having strong social skills allows people to build meaningful relationships with other people and develop a stronger understanding of themselves and others.

First, understand that a lot of our emotional world has a social component to it. For example, emotions such as love, guilt, rejection, and embarrassment are almost strictly social emotions (they rarely exist outside the context of our relationships with others).

To build healthy relationships it's important that we are attuned to other people's emotions, especially how they respond to our actions and speech.

If your actions cause negative emotions in other people, then that can hurt a relationship and your ability to connect with others in a meaningful way.

Cultivating positive emotions – like joy, optimism, excitement, and humor – is key toward bonding with others in a strong and lasting way.

Have you ever walked into a room of people who are depressed or stressed out, and you immediately begin to feel depressed and stressed too? This is an example of emotional contagion, which is the idea that our emotions can often spread to others like a virus.

In the same way that other people's emotions affect us, our emotions affect other people. So if you walk around life with a generally positive attitude, that is going to rub off on those you interact with (but you have to first have your mind in order).

The social skills aspect of emotional intelligence is about becoming an "emotional leader" of sorts. But you need to practice turning negative people around by first being positive in yourself.

5. Motivation

Intrinsic motivation is another pillar of emotional intelligence. Emotionally intelligent people are motivated by things beyond external rewards like fame, money, recognition, and acclaim.

Instead, they have a passion to fulfill their own inner needs and goals. They seek internal rewards, experience flow from being totally in tune with activity, and pursue peak experiences.

Those who are competent in this area tend to be action-oriented. They set goals, have a high need for achievement, and are always looking for ways to do better. They also tend to be very committed and are good at taking initiative.

Ways To Develop Your Emotional Intelligence

Emotional intelligence is something that comes naturally to some people, but not everyone. It's possible to improve your emotional intelligence with practice and effort.

Here are ways to develop your emotional intelligence.

1. Manage your negative emotions

When you're able to manage and reduce your negative emotions, you're less likely to get overwhelmed. Easier said than done, right? Try this: If someone is upsetting you, don't jump to conclusions. Instead, allow yourself to look at the situation in a variety of ways. Try to look at things objectively so you don't get riled up as easily. Practice mindfulness at work, and notice how your perspective changes.

Negative emotion is simply part of the full package that is emotion. Negative emotions are a result of negative events that occur in our lifetime e.g. sadness, grief, anger. We as humans can't avoid it. Therefore we must learn to manage it and ensure it does not impact us negatively.

2. Be mindful of your vocabulary.

Focus on becoming a stronger communicator in the workplace. Emotionally intelligent people tend to use more specific words that can help communicate deficiencies, and then they immediately work to address them. Had a bad meeting with your boss? What made it so bad, and what can you do to fix it next time? When you can pinpoint what's going on, you have a higher likelihood of addressing the problem, instead of just stewing on it.

3. Practice empathy

Be open-minded to the feelings of others; One of the hallmarks of emotional intelligence is empathy. Try to understand what others are feeling. Put yourself in their shoes. Try to look at an issue from a different perspective. It helps to be accommodating. To reach decisions that are beneficial to all. In communication, it helps you to be open-minded. Life is rarely black and white, there are many greys in between. Listen to debates and discussions on television and online.

Centering on verbal and non-verbal cues can give you invaluable insight into the feelings of your colleagues or clients. Practice focusing on others and walking in their shoes, even if just for a moment. Empathetic statements do not excuse unacceptable behavior, but they help remind you that everyone has their issues.

4. Bounce back from adversity

Everyone encounters challenges. It's how you react to these challenges that either sets you up for success or puts you on the track to full-on meltdown mode. You already know that positive thinking will take you far. To help you bounce back from adversity, practice optimism instead of complaining. What can you learn from this situation? Ask constructive questions to see what you can take away from the challenge at hand.

5. Be Responsible for your behavior

A lot of people never take responsibility for their behavior. There is a tendency to blame others for our own mistakes and flaws. But to improve your emotional intelligence you must learn to come to terms with your behavior and emotions. This is not about right or wrong, it is about accepting and coming to terms with your feelings and actions.

Though it is now an accepted fact that our environment plays a great deal in our behaviors in the end as humans it is our choice to act on our desires and emotions. Be honest with yourself and accept that your actions belong to you and you alone. You choose how you react to situations and various people. Only when you accept that can you begin to improve on the aspect you believe needs improvement.

6. Think Positive

You are what you think. Your relationships, your health, and a lot more are affected by what you think. Thinking impacts your health negatively, in a team it demoralizes your teammates, it makes a stressful situation even worse because it robs you of the ability to think rationally to find solutions.

This is not to say you should ignore the reality of the situation you are facing but when you attempt to be positive it frees your mind to the available possibilities. This is not something that happens overnight, it is a constant work in progress.

7. Stay In The Moment

When we're stressed out and overwhelmed, it's easy to think that everything negative that happens is because of something we did or didn't do. We can't control what happened before, but we can control how we react to our feelings now. Try not to dwell on the past; instead, focus on what you want your future to be like.

8. Identify Your Triggers

Negative emotions like guilt and shame aren't logical (meaning they don't make sense), but they feel completely real and important at the time when you're feeling them. To improve your EQ skills, try keeping a journal where you record every time an uncomfortable emotion comes up and then write about why that emotion occurred based on specific events or triggers.

9. Use Assertive Communication Style

Assertive communication style is communicating with others so that you show respect for their opinions without letting them step over your rights, needs, and personal boundaries. It helps you speak up for yourself without creating any interpersonal conflicts or tension among the team members.

10. Respond Instead of Reacting

When you decide without considering its consequences, you're reacting. On the other hand, when you pause for a second, take a quick analysis of the situation, and act consciously, you're responding.

Impulsive decisions in a situation of conflict can lead to bigger problems in your career. So think of the resolution each time you're in such a situation and make a conscious choice.

CHAPTER TWELVE
EMOTIONAL INTELLIGENCE ASSESSMENT

1. You're on an airplane that suddenly hits extremely bad turbulence and begins rocking from side to side. What do you do?

   A. Continue to read your book or magazine, or watch the movie, trying to pay little attention to the turbulence.

   B. Become vigilant for an emergency, carefully monitoring the cabin staff and reading the emergency instructions card.

   A little of both A and B.

   Not sure – you probably never noticed.

2. You are in a meeting when a colleague takes credit for work that you have done. What do you do?

   A. Immediately and publicly confront the colleague over the ownership of your work.

   B. After the meeting, take the colleague aside and tell her that you would appreciate it in the future that she credits you when speaking about your work.

   C. Nothing, it's not a good idea to embarrass colleagues in public.

   D. After the colleague speaks, publicly thank her for referencing your work and give the group more specific details about what you were trying to accomplish.

3. You are a customer service representative and are speaking to an extremely angry client on the phone. What do you do?

    A. Hang up. You aren't paid to take abuse from anyone.

    B. Listen to the client and rephrase what you gather he is feeling.

    C. Explain to the client that he is being unfair, that you are only trying to do your job, and you would appreciate it if he wouldn't get in the way of this.

    D. Tell the client you understand how frustrating this must be for him, and offer a specific thing you can do to help him get his problem resolved.

4. You are a college student who had hoped to get an A on an exam that was important for your future career aspirations. You have just found out you made a "C" What do you do?.

    A. Sketch out a specific plan for ways to improve your mark and resolve to follow it through.

    B. Decide you do not have what it takes to make it in that career.

    C. Tell yourself it doesn't matter how well you do in the course; concentrate instead on the other classes where your marks are higher.

    D. Go and discuss your results with your teacher and try to talk him into giving you a better mark.

5. You are a manager in an organization that is trying to encourage respect for racial and ethnic diversity. You overhear someone telling a racist joke. What do you do?

    A. Ignore it – the best way to deal with these things is not to react.

    B. Call the person into your office and explain that their behavior is inappropriate and is grounds for disciplinary action if repeated.

  C. Speak up on the spot, saying that such jokes are inappropriate and will not be tolerated in your organization.

  D. Suggest to the person who told the joke that he attend a diversity training course.

6. You are an insurance salesman calling on prospective clients. You have had no success with your last fifteen clients. What do you do?

  A. Call it a day and go home early to miss rush-hour traffic.

  B. Try something new in the next call, and keep plugging away.

  C. List your strengths and weaknesses to identify what may be undermining your ability to sell.

  D. Sharpen up your resume.

7. You are trying to calm down a colleague who has worked herself into a fury because the driver of another car has swerved dangerously close to her car. What do you do?

  A. Tell her to forget about it – she's OK now and it is no big deal.

  B. Put on some of her favorite music and try to distract her.

  C. Join her in criticizing the other driver.

  D. Tell her about a time something like this happened to you, and how angry you felt until you saw the other driver was on the way to the hospital.

8. A discussion between you and your partner has escalated into a shouting match. You are both upset and, in the heat of the argument, have started making personal attacks that neither of you means. What s'the best thing to do?

  A. Agree to take a 20-minute break before continuing the discussion.

  B. Go silent, regardless of what your partner says.

C. Say you are sorry and ask your partner to apologize too.

D. Stop for a moment, collect your thoughts, then restate your side of the case as precisely as possible.

9. You have been given the task of managing a team that has been unable to come up with a creative solution to a work problem. What's the first thing you do?
   A. Draw up an agenda, call a meeting and allot a specific period to discuss each item.

   B. Organize an off-site meeting aimed specifically at encouraging the team to get to know each other better.

   C. Ask each person individually for ideas about how to solve the problem

   D. Have a brainstorming session, encouraging each person to say whatever comes to mind, no matter how wild.

10. You have recently been assigned a young manager in your team and have noticed that he appears to be unable to make the simplest of decisions without seeking advice from you. What do you do?

    A. Accept that he 'doesn't have what it takes to succeed around here' and find others on your team to take on his tasks.

    B. Get an HR manager to talk to him about where he thinks his future within the organization might lie.

    C. Purposely give him lots of complex decisions to make so that he will become more confident in the role.

    D. Engineer an ongoing series of challenging but manageable experiences for him, and make yourself available to act as his mentor

HOW DOES SELF-AWARENESS RELATES TO EMOTIONAL INTELLIGENCE

Emotional intelligence starts with emotional self-awareness. Self-awareness requires accepting emotional experiences as real, valid, legitimate aspects of human experience and instead of denying emotional responses or reactions to situations, using the emotional information to make better decisions and take actions. Emotional self-awareness allows an individual to feel better or to do things better depending on the actions he or she takes in response to emotions, as opposed to reacting merely to soothe or stifle unpleasant and intense emotional sensations.

Consider your own experience of converting fear into competence. Every child is told to avoid a hot stove, and on occasion, an overly-curious child burns his fingers on the stove-only to learn a very painful lesson. However, most of us do not cower in fear whenever we walk into a kitchen. We recognize that the fear of being burned turns into a well-informed caution and respect for the power of the flame. As a result of our own experience, and recognizing our emotional response, we process fear and turn it into the ability to perform a task: we respond with caution to an open flame rather than react out of fear to the possibility that we might get burned.

While emotions are subtle and combine in complex ways, it is useful to model emotions on a simple "palate" from which more complex emotions are construed. The spectrum of emotions follows the pattern:

Anger - Sadness - Fear - Happiness

That is, this model suggests that anger is closer in modality to sadness than fear; fear is closer to sadness than anger, and happiness is closer to fear than sadness.

To understand your emotional response to an event, think of a goal you highly prize. It could be seeking a promotion; it could be recognition for a job well done; it could be the success of your firm. Make sure it's an important goal to you.

Now imagine someone outside threatens your goal, using an unfair tactic. A coworker misrepresents a situation and costs you a promotion. A competitor sends in senior managers to steal one of your key accounts. In this situation, you most likely feel anger directed toward the other person because they intentionally and somewhat maliciously did something to block your goal. In general, anger is directed toward an agent, another person or group, who actively blocks our goal.

Compare this to the feeling you would have when that same goal is not available, but there is no one to blame. Maybe the promotion vanished because of a downturn in the economy. Maybe your key account simply does not need your services anymore. Since no agent actively blocked your goal, your goal is now simply lost. Most likely you feel sadness at the loss since your goal is not attainable but it is not anyone's fault (not even your own).

Suppose now your goal is in an unknown state. Maybe it's threatened by another person, or maybe you're waiting for news as to whether the customer will continue to use your services. In that uncertain situation in which you are waiting for the resolution you most likely experience fear of your goal being lost, which will later settle into sadness or anger when you become certain of the outcome. Fear involves having your goal in an uncertain, possibly positive, and possibly negative, state.

Finally, assume you get surprise news that your goal has been met. Your promotion has been agreed upon by your managing partners and will be granted three months early. Or your key account has decided to double their projected work with you because of an upturn in the economy. With your goal unexpectedly facilitated and achieved, you most likely feel happiness given the unexpected result. Happiness occurs when a goal we have worked toward is achieved, and the sudden or surprising nature of the news can create excitement; just as sudden news can create anxiety that leads to sadness in the negative case.

This exercise provides insight into how your emotions inform you about your circumstances and can guide your response. If you are angry, for example, the questions you ask yourself include: Who are you angry with? What goal did he or she block? To resolve the situation, can the offender modify his or her behavior? Do you reorient your goals?

This level of self-awareness will make emotions more valuable, even integral to your decision-making. Emotions are not to be avoided, but rather embraced as essential tools to allow managers to make better decisions.

THE IMPORTANCE OF BECOMING EMOTIONALLY SELF-AWARE

Emotional self-awareness is the foundational competency of the Emotional Intelligence (EI) model I have worked with for over a decade. This competency provides a solid base upon which to build and enhance Emotional Intelligence competencies including emotional self-management, emotional self-motivation, empathy, and nurturing relationships. Yet many of us go through our day unaware and very accepting of the emotional roller coaster daily events evoke. And without recognizing where we are expending our emotional energy, it becomes difficult to progress to developing other EI competencies.

As we all deal with stress daily, we become accustomed to the pressures and hardly notice when the heat is turned up. Our stress levels rise when we experience negative emotions and are unable to cope with the challenges of our environment. We've all heard of the damaging effects of stress, but what's surprising is that many people don't realize they are experiencing negative emotions. If you don't know what emotion you're feeling, you don't have the information you need to decide whether to stay in that emotion or change or transform it.

Without the awareness of the importance of emotions, we do not have insight into how our responses to negative feelings are affecting us and those around us. On a personal level, negative emotions spark a cascade of 1400 biochemical events, some of which result in physiological changes such as increased adrenaline, heart rate, blood pressure, and cortisol (the stress hormone). This negatively affects your physical energy, mental clarity, and personal effectiveness. Experiencing these negative emotions can cause us to become defensive, short with people, and sometimes angry. And when others observe this response, we can lose their valuable suggestions, insight, and help as they start avoiding us.

Even with the awareness of how important emotions are, people may experience personal anxiety or hesitancy to openly advocate for developing EI skills. Some of my workshop participants have reported significant benefits from using the EI techniques I teach, yet, particularly in a technical field such as Engineering, are hesitant to promote an EI program for others. While there certainly is a bell-shaped curve of those who do or don't make a choice to benefit from the development of EI skills, not providing the opportunity is an opportunity lost for everybody.

What Can You Do?

Start by identifying typical situations at work or at home in which you feel negative emotions such as anxiety, frustration, anger, fear, or sadness. For example, you may feel frustrated when people who have important information don't show up for a meeting. Or you may feel angry when you see a certain person because he always wastes your time. Or you may feel anxiety when your boss approaches you about a particular project. Or you may feel depressed on Sunday night when you think about all the work facing you in the coming week. Identifying these situations helps you realize those events that trigger negative emotions.

Next, pay attention to and name the emotions the identified triggers evoke. Also recognize and name the positive emotions you experience during fun times such as playing with a puppy, sharing dinner with friends, or just sitting in the sunshine. Start developing an emotional vocabulary and expand upon it as the occasion permits.

Create a baseline of where you are expending your emotional energy now. Draw a four-box grid, labeling the two right boxes as positive emotions and the two left as negative emotions. Label the upper two boxes as high-energy emotions and the lower two low-energy emotions. Recall the day's activities, interactions, and events. For each, identify your emotion and write the emotion in the appropriate box on the grid, noting how long you were in the emotion. For example, hesitant would lie in the lower-left box while anger would lie in the upper-left box. Peaceful would lie in the lower right box and excited in the upper right box. Annoyed, depending on your level of annoyance, would lie somewhere in the left two boxes.

When you finish you will have an emotional map of your day. You were in the zone of peak performance if the frequency and duration of your emotions lie on the right side of the grid. If they lie on the left side, you are in a stress zone. As you develop your EI skills, periodically recreate this map. Over time you will want to see yourself more frequently in the two right quadrants by choosing to transform negative emotions into positive, productive emotions.

CONCLUSION

The journey of self-awareness is worthwhile. Among an abundance of benefits, greater self-knowledge leads to more connection, purpose, better wellbeing, and improved relationships.

Even more, hopefully, you now feel equipped with the tools and understanding to start a fruitful, and purposeful approach to introspection. As a final note, I'd like you to remember that, from this very moment until your last breath, you are the one person you'll spend every waking moment with.

Why not learn about you as if you were someone else, all your dreams, desires, fears, tendencies, and traits? In exploring this in yourself, and becoming self-aware, whilst being curious, you may be surprised to uncover deep riches you never knew you had, skills you didn't realize you possessed, and qualities that remind you of your inherent beauty.

The encouraging part is that studies have shown that having even the basic information about our core is a great enough starting point for unlocking the benefits of self-awareness.

Self-awareness tells us what we should be doing for being happy and successful, yet we tend to suppress that knowledge and do things under the influence of circumstances. Gradually our core nature gets buried under various layers of compulsions, compromise, pretense, and sometimes even ignorance. We get into a life gear that's more about chasing and less about living. We get so entangled in the games of survival that we end up fighting against ourselves as opposed to teaming up with our strengths and winning any battle that comes our way.

The more layers we have given way to, the harder it is to unfold them and uncover our true selves. But with patience and practice, we all can meet our cores and change our lives for the better.

We welcome questions or comments.

Please contact me or visit my Website:

Suzanne M. Howard

suzhoward@yahoo.com

www.suzannemhoward.com

If you enjoyed this book and you think it will
benefit others, please take a few moments to
write a review on your favorite store,
and refer it to your friends.

.

REFERENCES

https://www.theladders.com/career-advice/the-power-of-self-awareness-how-to-build-successful-teams

https://mindfithypnosis.com/who-am-i-self-identity/

https://www.trackinghappiness.com/why-self-awareness-important/

https://www.rylncoaching.com/post/self-awareness-the-key-to-being-a-more-impactful-and-successful-leader

https://www.trackinghappiness.com/why-self-awareness-important/

https://www.change-management-coach.com/self-awareness.html

https://www.kornferry.com/insights/this-week-in-leadership/what-is-emotional-self-awareness

https://www.lifehack.org/849510/be-self-aware

https://www.lifecoach-directory.org.uk/blog/2019/05/20/the-benefits-of-self-awareness-in-the-workplace

https://trainingindustry.com/articles/leadership/the-importance-of-self-awareness-in-leadership

https://www.forbes.com/sites/averyblank/2021/08/10/5-ways-you-can-use-your-self-awareness-to-demonstrate-strength/?sh=1898d87c6609

https://www.indeed.com/career-advice/career-development/what-is-self-awareness

https://www.trackinghappiness.com/why-self-awareness-important/

https://warwick.ac.uk/services/wss/topics/selfawareness

https://studentshare.org/environmental-studies/1692780-self-awareness-and-effective-communication

https://www.thinkerbase.net/communication-training-courses/self-awareness-is-vital-to-effective-communication/

https://www.marciewalker.com/emotional-intelligence-self-awareness/

https://welchlin.com/emotional-intelligence-self-awareness-emotional-intelligence/

https://www.change-management-coach.com/self-awareness.html